Village

in

THE CHILTERNS

Alan Charles

COUNTRYSIDE BOOKS
NEWBURY, BERKSHIRE

First published 1998
© Alan Charles 1998

COUNTRYSIDE BOOKS
3 Catherine Road
Newbury, Berkshire

ISBN 1 85306 497 1

Designed by Graham Whiteman
Maps and photographs by the author
Illustrations by Trevor Yorke

Produced through MRM Associates Ltd., Reading
Printed by Woolnough Bookbinding Ltd., Irthlingborough

Contents

INTRODUCTION   6

WALK

1   MARSWORTH (3½ miles)   8

2   LITTLE GADDESDEN (5 miles)   12

3   HALTON (5 miles)   16

4   PICCOTTS END (7 miles)   20

5   ASKETT (3½ miles)   25

6   LEE COMMON (5½ miles)   30

7   FLAUNDEN (6½ miles)   35

8   BLEDLOW (6 miles)   40

9   RADNAGE (3 miles)   45

10   BRADENHAM (3½ miles)   49

11   LITTLE MISSENDEN (4 miles)   53

12   WATLINGTON (6½ miles)   57

13   FINGEST (3 miles)   62

14   PENN (4½ miles)   66

AREA MAP SHOWING LOCATIONS OF THE WALKS

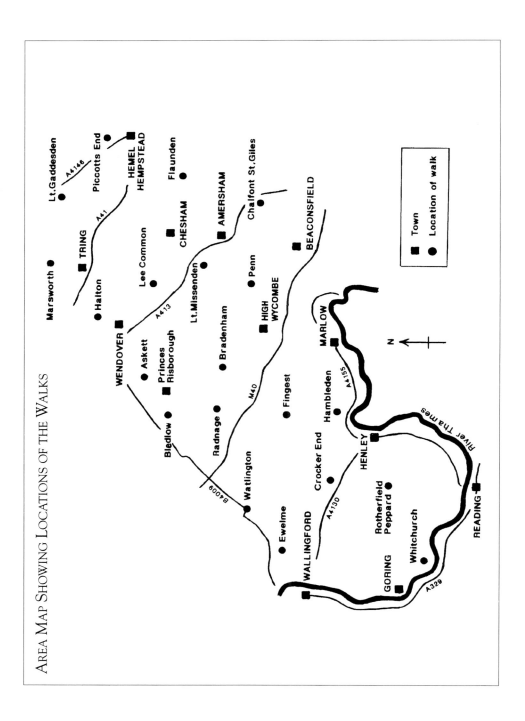

15	CHALFONT ST GILES (*7 miles*)	71
16	EWELME (*4½ miles*)	76
17	CROCKER END (*3½ miles*)	80
18	HAMBLEDEN (*4 miles*)	84
19	ROTHERFIELD PEPPARD (*4 miles*)	88
20	WHITCHURCH (*5½ miles*)	92

MAP SYMBOLS

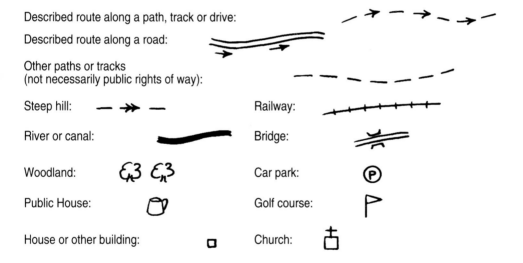

Described route along a path, track or drive:

Described route along a road:

Other paths or tracks
(not necessarily public rights of way):

Steep hill:

River or canal:

Woodland:

Public House:

House or other building:

Railway:

Bridge:

Car park:

Golf course:

Church:

Publisher's Note

We hope that you obtain considerable enjoyment from this book; great care has been taken in its preparation. Although at the time of publication all routes followed public rights of way or permitted paths, diversion orders can be made and permissions withdrawn.

We cannot of course be held responsible for such diversion orders and any inaccuracies in the text which result from these or any other changes to the routes nor any damage which might result from walkers trespassing on private property. We are anxious though that all details covering the walks are kept up to date and would therefore welcome information from readers which would be relevant to future editions.

Introduction

If those living in the Chilterns in the early 1900s could have looked ahead to the later years of the century and beyond, they would surely have marvelled at all the changes that were destined to take place in the countryside: farmsteads that had for long been at the hub of country life converted to luxurious dwellings or equestrian centres; village shops and artisans' workshops all but disappeared and their buildings surviving as private houses.

The saving grace today is that many of us greatly value our rural heritage and seek to preserve it. No less so in the Chilterns where we enjoy a marvellous legacy of attractive villages and beautiful countryside. It is from these villages and through this countryside that the 20 walks in this book have been devised. To complete all of them is to absorb a whole spectrum of delights that the Chilterns has to offer!

The walks range from 3 to 7 miles in length and each should easily be accomplished in the space of one half-day (a long half-day in the case of the 7 mile walks!). The distances given are measured on the map and do not allow for the extra ground trodden when walking uphill or downhill. Each walk is circular and is illustrated by a sketch map, designed to guide you to the starting point and give a simple but accurate idea of the route to be taken. However, for those who like the benefit of detailed maps, the relevant Ordnance Survey sheet is very much recommended, especially for identifying the main features of views. You will find that 17 of the walks may be followed on the Explorer series of OS maps, sheets 2 and 3.

These are on a scale of 2½ inches to the mile and are valuable to the walker since they show public rights of way and other useful information in considerable detail. The remaining walks can be followed on Landranger maps 166 and 175. These are on a scale of 1¼ inches to the mile. Landranger maps 165, 175 and 176 may be used as alternatives to the Explorer maps, although they give less detail.

Compass bearings (in degrees relative to the magnetic north pole) are given in the text where they are thought to aid navigation. These bearings have the advantage of changing very little over the years – which cannot always be said of natural and man-made landmarks!

The Chiltern Hills being exactly as their name suggests, some climbing must be expected from time to time. Very steep uphill paths are shown on the sketch maps by dual arrowheads, while general hilliness is intimated in the introduction to each walk. Some of the walks are largely without hills, while others include long stretches of flatness. Although difficult paths have been avoided whenever possible, it should be remembered that conditions can vary throughout the seasons and over the years. Problems are minimal in the Chilterns thanks to the many voluntary and statutory groups that have set themselves the task of clearing and waymarking paths and rebuilding stiles.

This brings us to the motor car. The lifeblood of any village is its inhabitants, and the Chilterns has an abundance of villagers who really care for their environment. Therefore, readers are asked to respect the villagers' way of life and to use the utmost discretion when parking vehicles. Car parking locations are indicated in the text – but if they are full, or for some reason unusable, please ensure that you park your vehicle in such a way as not to be a nuisance to those who live close by. Many of the walks commence from the village inn where, it must be stressed, parking is only for patrons. Please let the landlord know if you intend to leave your car at the pub while on the walk; some pubs close their car parks when the pub itself is closed, and you may find your car on the wrong side of the gate when you return from the walk!

In giving suggestions for eating out, I have included public houses and tea rooms lying on or within easy reach of the walks, and those that I have visited have been given the most detail. It is worth remembering, though, that pub management – and with it menus and ambience – can change during the tenure of a book like this. There are a few factors about pubs that are often overlooked. The most popular ones can be very busy at weekends, and so it may be worthwhile phoning ahead to reserve a table. On Sundays some pubs concentrate much of their energy on roast lunches and main meals, and it may not be possible for you to buy a snack (sandwiches for example) on that day. Some landlords are happy for customers to eat their own food in the garden if they are buying drinks; but some take the opposite view! So do please check first. Of tea rooms there is less to say, except that they can have the annoying habit of closing when you need them most – at tea time! So an early start to your walk may be advisable.

Whichever walk you choose (and I hope you will try them all) and wherever you eat and drink, do have a great day out in this superb area of Southern England.

Alan Charles

MARSWORTH

Length: 3½ miles

Getting there: Marsworth is 2 miles north of Tring and can be approached from the town along Brook Street (Ivinghoe direction) by the Robin Hood pub. Go straight on over the B488 at the first crossing and turn right into the B489 at the second, passing Tringford reservoir en route. Cross the Grand Union Canal by the White Lion pub, Startop's End (unless you have opted to start the walk here – see below) and turn first left for the village (Vicarage Road).

Parking: It is possible to park at Marsworth, either along the roadside or, for customers, in the car park of the Red Lion. If you choose to start and finish the walk by the canal at Startop's End (point 2), you could, for a small charge, leave your car in the British Waterways car park opposite the White Lion.

Maps: OS Explorer 2 Chiltern Hills North or Landranger 165 Aylesbury and Leighton Buzzard area (GR 920146).

Fortunately for Marsworth, its heart lies well off the B489, far enough to preserve the peacefulness of its location. Here you will find, in its own small way, the basic ingredients of the English village: pub, church, old cottages and manor house. The Grand Union Canal passes close by, beautiful here but unnoticed by visitors that descend on nearby Startop's End – where anchored boats, huge reservoirs and

---

FOOD and DRINK

There are four pubs on or close to the walk. The Red Lion at Marsworth is well known for its unsophisticated food, which includes delicious home-cooked ham. Telephone: 01296 668366. The White Lion and the Anglers Retreat at Startop's End offer a wide range of snacks and meals every day (roast lunch only on winter Sundays at the Anglers Retreat). Telephone: 01442 822325 and 01442 822250. The Half Moon at Wilstone (just off the walk) is especially recommended for its atmosphere and good food – which includes haggis imported from Scotland! Telephone: 01442 826410. At Wilstone the village shop sells hot and cold snacks. The Charlotte Tea Rooms overlooking the canal at Startop's End is open from 8 am to 8 pm every day. So you are spoilt for choice along this walk!

---

a good choice of refreshment houses add to the attraction of the canal.

A walk that includes a length of canal towpath is bound to be a winner! Here the choice is one mile of the Aylesbury Arm, a peaceful 'branch line' from 'Marsworth Junction'. Leaving the canal near Wilstone (a good stop-off for its pub and shop) the walk circulates around fields and farmsteads and meets the little river Ousel as it flows towards Marsworth. If you enjoy seeing the Chiltern Hills without the necessity of climbing, this walk will be to your liking!

THE WALK

❶ From the Red Lion go uphill to the road junction by the church. Turn right there into Church Lane and join a concrete drive on the left just beyond the Old Manor, a fine timber-framed house. When the drive soon turns right, go straight on across a parking area and through a gate. Passing between a bungalow and a stable, soon go over a stile on the right where the fields connect. On entering a corner after 25

yards, cross a rail into a small triangular piece of 'wasteland', then cross a succession of two fields towards the canal (190° in the first field). If you go half-left across the second field, you should arrive in its far corner by the canal bridge.

❷ Don't go under the bridge but climb a flight of steps and cross the canal on a footbridge. The Charlotte Tea Rooms is now in close range, as are the White Lion and the Anglers Retreat – also the British Waterways car park (alternative starting point). Having crossed the footbridge turn right onto the canal towpath. Passing the garden of the White Lion, go along the towpath of the canal to 'Marsworth Junction' and turn left into the Aylesbury Arm.

❸ Walk the towpath of the Aylesbury Arm for about a mile, passing three brick-built canal bridges. The original plan to link this 6¼ mile branch of the canal to the river Thames at Abingdon came to nothing. In 1964 it was threatened with closure, but the Aylesbury Canal Society came to the rescue and secured its future.

❹ A timber footbridge crossing the canal marks the point of departure for Wilstone, and a left turn here into a footpath will, if you so desire, take you to the excellent Half Moon pub or the village shop in no time at all. To continue on the walk however, you should go over the footbridge to a field opposite. Cross this field in the direction slightly left of a twin-poled electricity pylon (320°). Go over a stile and footbridge there and cut off the sharp corner of the next field to another stile. Turn right immediately

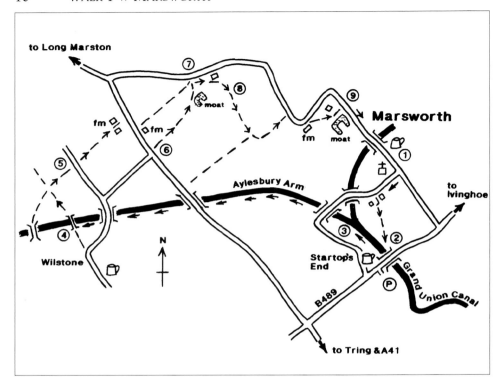

and, passing under the power line, join a tree-shaded track between fields.

❺ Turn right into a road from the far end of the track and leave it for a stile on the left after a few yards. Following a hedge and ditch on your left make your way along the field-edge to a stile at the far end, not far from a large green barn. From the stile go forward through the yard of College Farm and turn right onto a road.

❻ Leave the road at a junction after 200 yards, crossing a stile on the left opposite Tring road. As you walk the left-hand edge of a large field you have a sweeping view of the Chiltern Hills, including the kite flyers'

Ivinghoe Beacon! When you are very nearly at the far left-hand corner, go over a stile into the adjacent field. Make your way across this field – slightly left of your previous direction – to a stile and gate in the far corner (10°).

❼ Pass between an earth mound and a moat and cross a stile and footbridge on the left after a few yards. Turn right into a bridleway immediately and soon cross another footbridge. Don't step into the road there but go over a stile on the right and walk through a garden parallel to the little river Ousel. Follow the left bank of the river through this garden and the next (if you experience difficulty in passing from one garden to the next, you may need to cross the river from the first garden and recross to the second). After 80 yards in the second garden cross the river from a corner and enter a field on the right. Go half-left across this large field, cutting off its rounded corner in the process.

❽ With the river meandering under trees on the left, soon follow the field-edge and enter the next field from the far corner. Turn left through a gap immediately onto a concrete drive, following this to a road. Turn right in the road and leave it when it soon turns left. Go through a kissing-gate at the corner and turn left immediately to pass between a large metal barn and a hedge. From the far end of the barn go half-right across a field to a stile (near a farm gate)

PLACES of INTEREST

This a great area for further exploration: **Startop's End Reservoir** for bird watching and waterside walking; **Pitstone Wharf** for canal trips and refreshments; **Ivinghoe Beacon** for hill climbing and kite flying!

---

and, veering slightly left, continue to another stile at the roadside. Lower End Garage is nearby.

❾ Turn right into the road (the same road as previously) and follow this back to the canal and Marsworth village. The moat that you pass along this final leg of the walk once surrounded an early manor house. Three sides of the moat remain but the house has long since disappeared.

The Grand Union Canal at Startop's End.

LITTLE GADDESDEN

Length: 5 miles

Getting there: Little Gaddesden is signposted from Hudnall Corner (1½ miles) and Dagnall (2½ miles) on the A4146 between Hemel Hempstead and Leighton Buzzard.

Parking: Cars can be parked in Church Road near the northern end of the green. Customers at the Bridgewater Arms may wish to leave their cars in the pub car park while on the walk, but they should check first with the landlord. To commence the walk turn left when leaving either the pub building or Church Road. Alternatively, you could choose to start the walk from the Bridgewater Monument (point 7), leaving your car in the adjacent parking area.

Maps: OS Explorer 2 Chiltern Hills North or Landranger 165 Aylesbury and Leighton Buzzard area (GR 993134).

If the residents of Little Gaddesden need a buffer from the Ringshall road and the trees of the Ashridge estate, they have it in their ½ mile long green. Here the passer-by can admire their fine houses, which once accommodated workers from the estate. In the 1840s this labour force amounted to no less than 700 persons. Whether they had time to enjoy this 'first garden village of Hertfordshire', I'm not sure!

Included in this walk is the great variety of interest for which Ashridge Park is

FOOD and DRINK

The Bridgewater Arms is close to the green, where the walk starts. Fresh and seasonal food is served every lunchtime and evening, with choices ranging from ploughman's and filled jacket potatoes to rabbit in gin and prune sauce! The menu card also includes an informative outline of the history and wildlife of the area. Telephone: 01442 842408. A National Trust tea garden is situated halfway along the walk and is open on summer weekends.

famous: there are impressive vistas and shady woodlands, a fine castellated house and a 100 ft granite monument. Much of the estate is owned by the National Trust, who have established an information room, gift shop and tea garden – all conveniently placed near the mid-point of the walk.

THE WALK

❶ A long tarmac path runs the length of the green at Little Gaddesden alongside the gardens. With these gardens on your left walk the path all the way to Hudnall Lane at a road junction. Turn right here and cross the road junction to a footpath sign (near a seat) opposite. This leads you into a good path under trees and soon downhill to the left of a fence. From a kissing-gate lower down, follow the meandering path into a wide grassy valley – Golden Valley.

❷ Cross the valley half-right to a wide gap opposite (not seen initially), then go uphill to a drive. If you find yourself on a track at the top, simply turn right to join the drive. There is a bend in the drive at this point,

The fine castellated house at Ashridge Park.

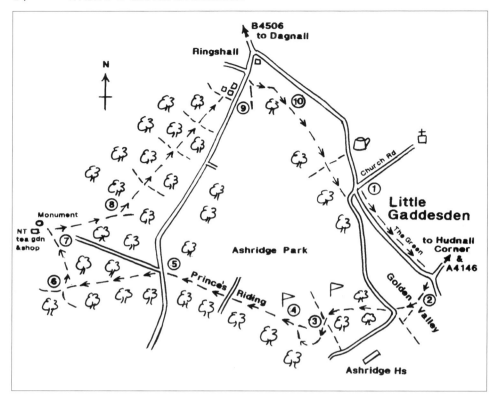

and a view of Ashridge House. Replacing an earlier monastic building, the present house was completed in the early 1800s by the 7th Earl of Bridgewater. It now serves its time as a management college. The gardens and woodland behind the house are open to the public on weekend afternoons in summer. So extensive and attractive are they that a separate visit is required! Cross the drive to a National Trust waymark post on the right-hand side of the bend and climb the bank to a horse track under trees (260°). An expanse of playing fields will then come into view about 20 yards to the left. The track enjoys a sequence of woodland and open areas before circulating clockwise around – and within 30 yards of – a golf course fairway.

❸ At one point you will have sight of Ashridge House and Prince's Riding (a wide grassy break in the trees) at one and the same time, with the Bridgewater Monument at the far end of the Riding. You should maintain your clockwise rotation – with the fairway remaining in view on your right – until you emerge onto the Riding itself. Your point of contact with the Riding will be about 50 yards from its fenced right-hand extremity and by a 'No Galloping' sign.

❹ Turn left into the Riding and follow its straight course in the direction of the monument, crossing a metalled forestry drive in the process and, after a further ⅓ mile, meeting a public road from a gate and fence.

❺ Assuming your back is to the gate, branch half-left as you cross the road and join a bridleway under trees. This is identified by a waymark post and blue arrow about 30 yards to the left of a metalled drive (you could alternatively go straight along the drive, all the way to the monument, but you may be accompanied by motorists!). Ignoring crossings and branches, keep straight on along the bridleway until, after ½ mile, you are close to a field ahead, near its left-hand extremity.

❻ Turn right and follow a track all the way to the National Trust information centre and tea garden, keeping parallel to the field edge as you go. The monument commemorates the 3rd Duke of Bridgewater, one-time owner of Ashridge, for his pioneering efforts in the early days of the canal age. He is often referred to as 'the Father of Inland Navigation' or 'the Canal Duke'. For a modest fee you can climb the 172 steps of the monument and enjoy an outstanding view across the Chilterns.

❼ Refreshed and informed, you should resume the walk from the small pear-shaped green, with the drive ahead and the monument to the rear. Go half-left from this point, and, passing about 20 yards to the right of a pond, soon join a wide horse track under trees (80°). After passing another pond (on your right) keep straight on along this track and go half-left with it (40°) after ¼ mile, following it into a dip.

❽ You should now keep absolutely straight on for more than ½ mile until you are confronted by a garden fence. Turn right there, and, following an old garden wall, join the road at Ringshall.

❾ Turn left in the road and walk downhill to a small pumping station on the right, using the right-hand enbanked path for safety. Go through a kissing-gate just before the pumping station and join a level path running alongside a garden fence. Ignoring a half-right branch after about 75 yards, follow the fence to a stile and enter a wood.

❿ Keeping to the main path, leave the wood and continue forward along a metalled drive, by the entrance to Witchcraft Hill. If the Bridgewater Arms (or the nearby village shop) is your next preferred port of call, look for a path on the left 75 yards before Wychcroft Cottage (not Witchcraft Hill), and follow this up to the pub or shop. To return to the green at Little Gaddesden keep forward until you meet the drive to Ashridge House. Turn hairpin left here and go uphill to the green.

HALTON

Length: 5 miles

Getting there: Halton village is signposted from the A4011 along Chestnut Avenue, 1 mile north-east of Wendover.

Parking: Cars can be left in a layby near the canal bridge, or in the road on the airfield side of the village. If starting the walk from Wendover, a convenient street in which to park is Wharf Road, by the canal (see map and point 8).

Maps: OS Explorer 2 Chiltern Hills North or Landranger 165 Aylesbury and Leighton Buzzard area (GR 874101).

Halton is beautifully sited beside the Wendover Arm of the Grand Union Canal. The variety in size and shape of the houses, some with plaster panels illustrating harvest and other country scenes, is a reminder that Halton was once part of a Rothschild estate. Although the village is almost completely surrounded by the grounds of RAF Halton – the Rothschilds' successor since 1918 – this in no way detracts from the rural atmosphere of the village, to the casual observer at least.

After leaving the recreation grounds of RAF Halton the walk launches into a long but stimulating ascent through Wendover Woodland Park, with the reward of an outstanding view across Aylesbury Vale. The historic town of Wendover is visited at the halfway point and the walk concludes with a peaceful amble along the Wendover Canal – which you could well mistake for a Chiltern river!

THE WALK

❶ The walk starts from Halton's parish church, opposite the bus shelter and a short distance from the canal. Go through the churchyard gates and pass to the right of the church. Notice how the church is constructed: with blocks of 'clunch' (a hard chalk stone) pointed with tiny dashes of flint. The numerous graves of service personnel are a reminder of the RAF's long-established presence in the area. Leave the churchyard through a kissing-gate on the far side and turn left immediately, following the churchyard fence and with RAF 'married quarters' over to the right. Soon turn half-left under the trees (many pedestrians have simply continued straight on) and head for a waymark post beside a wide path – also under trees.

❷ Turn right on the path and, with the RAF recreation ground on the left, follow the path to its junction with a drive. Turning left there, and with the recreation ground now on both sides, stay with the drive as it accompanies trees on the right. On your way you will have a view of Halton airfield and a possible glimpse of Halton House through the trees. Built in 1884 and now an officers' mess, the house is one of seven Rothschild mansions that existed in the area at one time. When the drive turns right (on its way to the house) go over a stile in the fence on the left and walk uphill on a wide path under trees. When the path meets another drive turn left and go uphill to the A4011.

❸ Cross to a drive opposite, and, passing a lodge house, go through a gate into Wendover Woodland Park. Once owned by the Rothschild family, this vast area of woodland came into the hands of the Forestry Commission in 1939. The Commission has set out a number of trails, each with its own special interest. An example is the Firecrest Trail, where the tiniest of our birds, the rare firecrest, can be seen. Go straight on uphill along the wide track (not the narrow bridleway lower down on the right) and soon cross another bridleway.

❹ After ½ mile (measured from the road) a flight of steps by a low flint wall on the left ushers in a waymarked crossing-path. Keep forward here on the wide track for just 120 yards to the next waymarked Y-junction. Take the right-hand branch – the least steep branch – and keep forward along this. Ignore a path that crosses the track obliquely, and eventually find yourself at a marvellous viewpoint.

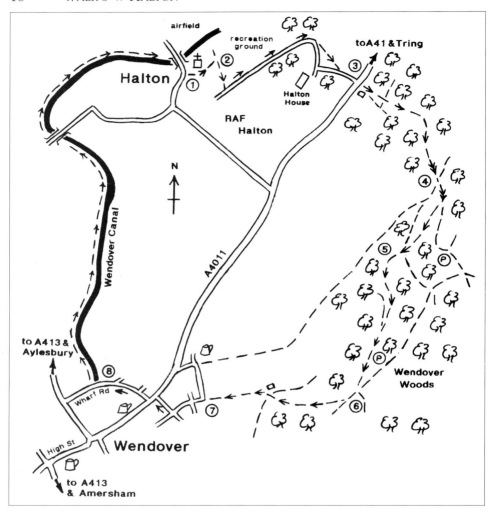

❺ From the viewpoint you can see the Vale of Aylesbury and the town of Wendover. Beyond Wendover stands Coombe Hill with its Boer War monument. Keeping forward again and ignoring all branches, you will in due course arrive at the summit of Wendover Woods, with an extensive picnic and parking area and a 'fitness trail' – from which, after all this climbing, you may now consider yourself well and truly exempt!

❻ Ignoring lesser paths, go forward from the picnic area (beyond a roughly surfaced turning circle) into a wide track, with the fitness trail running parallel on the right. Now take care: leave the track after only 75 yards (about 100 paces) and branch half-right downhill (260°) by exercise point number 2. A steeper descent follows and your path crosses a level track. It soon meets a rough drive by the entrance gates to a single large house. Turn half-left into this level drive – between hedges and with a field on the left – and follow this to a road and housing estate.

❼ Keep forward between the houses and turn right at the second crossing into Colet Road, by the post box. Having emerged from Colet Road go slightly left over the A4011 to Manor Road opposite and stay with this until it becomes Wharf Road. 'Wharf' is appropriate since it is here that you will find the start of the Wendover Canal (more correctly the Grand Union Canal, Wendover Arm!). Originally constructed to supply water to the summit level of the main canal at Marsworth, the Wendover Arm became a valued but short-lived asset to the town, for transporting goods far and wide. Owing to incurable leakage of water, the canal was abandoned in 1904. It has since become a haven for wildlife and a great place along which to walk.

❽ Before joining the towpath this is a good moment to explore the town and its refreshment houses. Simply keep forward in Wharf Road and turn left at the end. When you are happy come back to the canal and walk the towpath all the way back to Halton, which is at the second road bridge.

Cold Harbour Cottages, Wendover.

PICCOTTS END

Length: 7 miles

| Getting there: Piccotts End is 1 mile north of Hemel Hempstead. It is signposted from the Old Town Centre and from the A4146 by Gadebridge Park. | Parking: It is possible to park in the main street of the village. If you choose a spot near the Boar's Head pub you will enjoy the village to the full as you walk the first part of the route. The Boar's Head pub has a | car park for customers.

Map: OS Landranger 166 Luton, Hertford and surrounding area (GR 053088). |
| --- | --- | --- |

Previously on the main road out of Hemel Hempstead, Piccotts End now enjoys relative peace and quiet, thanks to the A4146 that bypasses the village. All the better to appreciate the superb houses and cottages with which the village is endowed.

The walk follows both the upper and lower levels of the Gade valley, firstly near the river itself, then on the heights around Briden's Camp. By Gaddesden Place a magnificent view of the valley opens up – before the walk descends to the conserved meadows at Water End. Climbing once more, in part steeply, the walk enjoys the valley from the west, and crosses cultivated fields near Potten End.

FOOD and DRINK

You could hardly do better than to lunch at the Boar's Head, Piccotts End! A good bar menu is available every day and includes anything from sandwiches and ploughman's to mixed grill, lasagne and chilli con carne. Telephone: 01442 240084. Along the walk the Red Lion at Water End follows the reliable Miller's Kitchen regime (telephone: 01442 213594), while the Crown and Sceptre at Briden's Camp offers an extensive menu every day (telephone: 01442 253250). The Coffee Shop at Hillier's Garden Centre serves meals and light refreshments – not just coffee! This is on the A4146 near Piccotts End. There is a tea room at Bingham's Park Children's Farm a little off the walk near Potten End.

THE WALK

❶ With the Boar's Head pub on your left, go along the main street for ¼ mile to a stile on the left just before the road humps. You will in the process pass a terrace of old timber-framed houses, a little beyond Church House. It was in one of these houses that a collection of 15th-century wall paintings was discovered in 1953. Although these paintings are not normally accessible for public viewing, their discovery has earned the village no small reputation. It is thought that together the houses may have served as a hostel for medieval pilgrims en route to the monastery at Ashridge.

❷ From the stile soon cross a footbridge over the Gade and turn right from a kissing-gate into the A4146. Go along the grass verge for 60 yards and cross the road to a gate and drive by the Three Valleys Water pumping station. Walk the drive almost as far as the next gate (there is a house beyond it) and pass through a kissing-gate on the right. Initially continuing in your previous direction, you should rotate clockwise around three sides of an enclosed area, with a metal fence on your right all the way. A kissing-gate will then set you on course parallel to the valley. The path meanders between the trees and a meadow before running more or less straight on along the lower edge of an arable field. Cross a stile in the far right-hand corner of this long field and keep forward to another stile.

❸ With a very fine house, Gaddesden Hall, on your right, continue forward through two more meadows and over the intervening stile. Leave the second meadow from its far right-hand corner (not down the slope in the near corner) and step onto a drive. With Gaddesden Hall now behind you, leave the drive immediately (it turns left here) by going forward on a narrow path. When you soon enter the fields keep straight on along their right-hand edge, passing a clump of tall trees as you go. Leave the second field at a stile and gate 50 yards before the far right-hand corner and resume your former direction, but now along a rough drive by the houses. Turn right on the road at the end (Potten End Hill) and right again at the A4146.

❹ You now have a short piece of busy road, mellowed by a lovely view across the river Gade. Turn left into Red Lion Lane – opposite the pub of that name – and join a bridleway on the right when the lane soon turns left. Follow the waverings of the bridleway and its left-hand hedge uphill between the fields, then turn left when on the level – where four fields meet. A waymark post at this point should instill confidence!

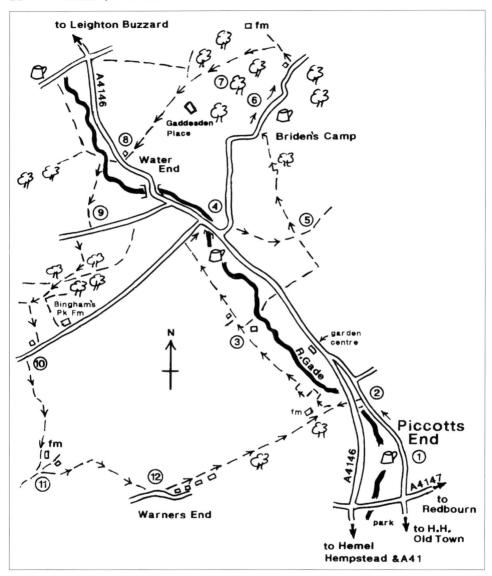

5 With another hedge on your left make your way gradually uphill to the near corner of a mature woodland (not the field corner). Turn left there (and enjoy a good view towards Hemel Hempstead) then right through a gap after walking 60 yards uphill. A farm track now takes you alongside the wood (the trees are on the right) and in the direction of houses at Briden's Camp. Turn left into a rough drive just before the houses, then right into a road – at a bend.

❻ After passing the Crown and Sceptre pub (or after leaving it!) follow the bends in the road and turn left by Almonds Cottage into the concrete drive to Grove and Home Farms. Signposted as a footpath the drive is about 100 yards beyond the second bend. Leave the drive at a stile and gate after 120 yards when the concrete terminates and cross the left-hand field towards a distant gap in the trees. This is quarter-right if your back is to the gate (250°). Gaddesden Place comes into view half-left as you cross the field to a gate and stile, and these connect you to the upper end of a meadow.

❼ Now take care! On leaving the gate, pass to the *left* of a deep pit – and don't be tempted onto a waymarked horse trail to the right of the pit. Then, briefly walking under trees, take a level route across a rough pasture to a gate on the far side (240°). This gate is 30 yards from the far left-hand corner of the pasture. Continuing forward from the gate – and with Gaddesden Place behind the trees on your left – cross the corner of a field to a stile. Now keep more or less straight on through a sequence of fields and over stiles all the way down to the right-hand group of houses at Water End, which should not be confused with Great Gaddesden, the village with the church tower. Your view of the valley as you descend is also enjoyed by Gaddesden Place. Originally completed in the 1770s by James Wyatt, this Palladian villa was rebuilt in 1905 following a fire. So what you now see of the house is not as old as you might have thought!

PLACES of INTEREST

Hemel Hempstead's Old Town Centre is a short drive away. It possesses a number of interesting old buildings, including shops and public houses. It overlooks **Gadebridge Park**, an attractive open space by the river Gade.

❽ All being well you should join the road by houses numbered 19 and 20. Cross to a gap between the houses opposite and soon go over two stiles to the meadows beyond. Turn right immediately and go down behind the gardens to the river Gade and over its footbridge. Turning left and crossing another footbridge (there is a pond on the right) soon go over a stile by an electricity pole. Continue in the same direction through a pasture, eventually joining a road from the far right-hand corner.

❾ Turn right at the road and cross a stile on the left after 60 yards, then head uphill to the mid-point of a wood. Ignoring all branches, proceed uphill through the wood (half-right at the start) on a wide path. At the top you will see the paddocks of Bingham's Park Children's Farm. If the tea room and shop are of interest keep forward along the farm track; if not, turn right immediately (from a bend in the track) and go through a hedge gap on the right. Cross the field along a level path in the direction of a distant, part-hidden house (240°); and having walked one third of the *total* field length turn left alongside a shortened hedge. With the hedge on your right soon go through a kissing-gate, then keep forward along a rough drive by the house, St Moritz, after which turn right at the road – Potten End Hill again.

⑩ When after 100 yards you see a pond on the right, cross the road to a signposted gate opposite and follow a hedge between fields to a stile. Keep straight on from the stile, downhill along the field edge and into a dip. Bearing half-left from a stile at the bottom, ascend the opposite slope along a wide track. Leave the track when it runs into a farmyard and keep forward in a field to its far left-hand corner. Turn right from the corner and follow the field edge parallel to a metalled farm drive.

⑪ Cross the drive just beyond the farm's entrance gates to the field edge opposite. Keep straight on along the left-hand edge of this field and the right-hand edge of the next, and go half-right from the far corner to join the adjacent field. Following a line of trees on the left, pass under electricity wires and eventually join Fennycroft Road.

⑫ Turn left along the road and soon cross a stile on the left, just prior to the houses. You now have a ¾ mile stretch of path, straight and true all the way to the A4146, firstly behind gardens, then alongside a wood and between fences, finally through a farm. After crossing the A4146 to the grass verge, turn right and soon left into a short path. And there you are – back at Piccotts End.

ASKETT

Length: 3½ miles

Getting there: Askett is a short distance from the A4010 between Princes Risborough and Great Kimble and is clearly signposted from that road.

Parking: It is possible to park off the main street in Crowbrook Road, near what was once the White Cross public house. If you choose to start the walk at Monks Risborough (point 6), you could park in the side road off the A4010.

Maps: OS Explorer 2 Chilterns Hills North or Landranger 165 Aylesbury and Leighton Buzzard area (GR 815052).

At first sight Askett appears as a small village with a pub, a few cottages and a large converted barn – nothing more. However, much of its glory is tucked away along Askett Lane, out of sight of the main street but on our return route.

The walk encompasses a stretch of the Chiltern escarpment that is breathtaking to say the least. From Great Kimble it climbs steadily to the lower slopes of Pulpit Hill. It skims Grangelands, a county nature reserve, and briefly joins the Ridgeway Trail. After descending to Longdown Hill (a road) it climbs once more – to the lower

---

FOOD and DRINK

The Three Crowns at Askett serves sandwiches and rolls (only) every lunchtime, and main meals in the evenings. Telephone: 01844 343041. The Red Lion at Whiteleaf serves meals every lunchtime and evening, with choices ranging from baguettes and home-made pies to a selection of fish dishes. Telephone: 01844 344476. The Plough at Cadsden is a short distance from the walk but access is along a busy, pavement-less road. The short drive to Princes Risborough is well worth making, since it will lead you to the Whiteleaf Cross pub (in Market Square), where excellent lunchtime meals are available (not Sundays or bank holidays). Telephone 01844 346834. You can park near the church or by Budgens' store.

---

slopes of Whiteleaf Hill. It samples the delights of Whiteleaf and Monks Risborough villages and returns to Askett along the incomparable Askett Lane.

THE WALK

❶ From a stile immediately to the right of the Three Crowns public house, follow the right-hand edge of a sequence of six fields, straight on and over the interconnecting stiles. Ignore a branch going half-left in the sixth field and continue to a double stile by a corner of a tree-shaded moat. The moat once surrounded the buildings of Old Grange Farm, which was originally owned by Missenden Abbey. The farmhouse and a fine 18th-century barn are situated beyond the trees. With the moat over to your left, cross the next field to a stile about 25 yards from the left-hand field corner. Pass under ornamental trees and cross a gravel drive to a stile; then aim for the opposite right-hand corner of a field, where there's a stile under an electricity pole. Going half-right (diagonally) across the next field, you will notice an extensive system of earthworks.

These are remnants of a medieval settlement which formed part of the nearby village of Great Kimble.

❷ Leave the field from a kissing-gate in the far right-hand corner and cross the road to a rough drive opposite. The drive is labelled as a bridleway and takes you uphill under trees, becoming a wide track in the process. Stay with the track for ½ mile, ignoring a kissing-gate on the left and a stile on the right as you go. Leave the track at a gate and stile on the right (it also has a dog gate) just beyond a field boundary and where the track narrows to a woodland path. After a few yards turn left along a chalky path (resuming your previous direction), and soon right into a dip. The wooded heights of Pulpit Hill will then be on your left. You are now on the Ridgeway Trail, which runs from Ivinghoe Beacon in Buckinghamshire to Overton Hill in Wiltshire, a distance of 85 miles.

❸ Climbing out of the dip, head towards a kissing-gate at the far left-hand corner of this open scrubby slope, ignoring a crossing path at the halfway point. In view half-left from the gate is the nature reserve of Grangelands, highly esteemed as a haven for wildlife – which includes flowers, birds and butterflies – and for the outstanding view that it offers! Turn right beyond the gate – with the Ridgeway Trail – then left with the trail immediately (it is labelled with acorn waymarks) and soon enter a field at a corner. Cross the field to the midpoint of a wood at the far end and descend a steep path to the road at Longdown Hill.

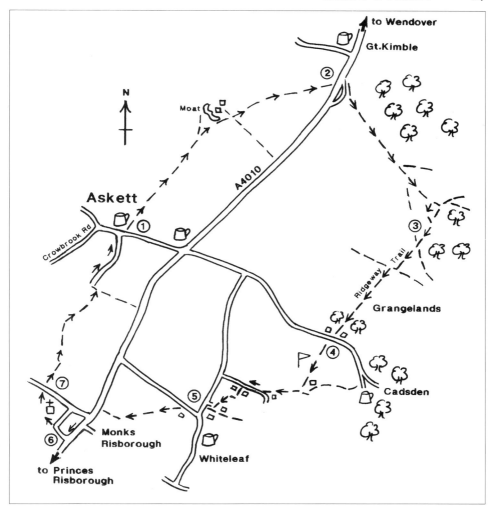

❹ Your short association with the Ridgeway Trail ends as you cross the road to the corner of a golf course. Go uphill alongside the course, following a hedge on the left as far as a thatched cottage, which you will notice is bastioned against those little white missiles! Cross the green half-right to a kissing-gate in the right-hand hedge, then look back at the superb view of Grangelands and Pulpit Hill! Keep forward from the hedge alongside the cricket pavilion to the drive beyond. Turn right into the drive and soon leave it for a path on the left – under trees between New Place and Woodpeckers. The path passes around the garden of Woodpeckers and joins a metalled drive between houses. When the drive soon curves right go forward across

Monks Risborough.

the grass and turn right into another drive, Thorns Lane, by Greensleeves.

❺ Turn left into the road ahead and right at the next junction, unless you have time to walk Whiteleaf's main street (Upper Icknield Way) directly ahead or to sample the Red Lion: both short, enjoyable diversions! From the road junction go down The Holloway for 60 yards to a point just beyond The White House and climb the bank to a narrow path under trees. Soon emerge from the trees and enter a field at its corner. After crossing the field straight on and downhill to a kissing-gate, pass to the right of a school and join the A4010 at Monks Risborough. Turn left there and cross Mill Lane to the war memorial; then keep forward along the A4010 to a side road. Here you will see some of Monks Risborough's cottages, including the one-time Nag's Head public house.

❻ Go along Burton Lane, and when this turns right to reveal another array of attractive cottages, keep forward along a pavement and follow this into the churchyard. The church is dedicated to St Dunstan, a 10th-century archbishop who included in his catalogue of skills those of statesman and metalworker. A modern sculpture in the south aisle shows him with blacksmith's tongs in hand, preparing to grip Satan's nose! The Chantry Chapel has a memorial window to Bishop Samuel Wilberforce, son of William Wilberforce, the anti slave-trade campaigner. Passing to the left of the church and glancing through the trees, you will see a restored 16th-century dovecote. The buildings of Place Farm, which once accompanied the dovecote, have sadly given way to a recreation ground.

❼ On leaving the churchyard cross Mill Lane to a path opposite. The path runs parallel to, but distant from, Courtmoor Close. It turns left beyond the houses and soon right to a footbridge and a field. Aim for a stile in the far left-hand corner of the field (20°), ignoring an earlier stile and a gate over to the left. Further stiles will take you under electricity wires and forward to a tree-shaded grassy area where, a little later, an old garden wall runs parallel on the left. Go left with the wall where a path crosses (not straight on into a private garden!) and follow this to Meadowcroft Farmhouse and Askett Lane. With its thatched and timber-framed houses, this is surely one of the most attractive roads along which to end a walk!

LEE COMMON

Length: 5½ miles

Getting there: From Chesham (by the public library) take the road signposted to Chartridge. Turn left for Lee Common 1½ miles beyond Chartridge, then right after a further ½ mile. The Chartridge road can also be accessed from the A413 1½ miles south of Wendover, where it is called Rocky Lane. Lee Common should not be confused with Lee Gate, The Lee or Lee Clump!

Parking: This is possible at the north end of the main street near its T-junction with the Chartridge/The Lee road. You could alternatively park at Great Missenden (it has a large car park) and start the walk there (point 9).

Maps: OS Explorer 2 Chiltern Hills North or Landranger 165 Aylesbury and Leighton Buzzard area (GR 907043).

Sitting on high ground well away from any busy road, Lee Common is a most delightful Chiltern retreat, with lovely flint-built cottages along its main street – Oxford Street. According to local knowledge the street was named thus by the Liberty family, owners of the Lee Manor Estate as well as the famous Regent Street shop. This gave them the satisfaction of possessing properties in both Regent Street and Oxford Street!

After descending Lee Manor Park the

FOOD and DRINK

There are no places for refreshment in Lee Common itself, but the Pheasant pub is a short distance from the walk at Ballinger Common. Telephone: 01494 837236. Great Missenden at the halfway point of the walk has four pubs along the High Street. The Waggon and Horses serves traditional pub food at reasonable prices as well as oriental dishes such as Thai curry. Telephone: 01494 862934. The tearoom at Drew's Bakery in the High Street – where the aroma of newly baked bread and cakes is difficult to resist – is open Monday to Friday until 4.30 pm, Saturday until 12.30 pm.

walk alternates between typical Chiltern woodland and open country. It enters Great Missenden along the beautifully maintained Church Street and leaves alongside a marvellous wild margin – alive with flowers and butterflies in summer. A series of level fields with views of distant woodlands and isolated cottages uplifts the spirit as the walk makes its final approach to Lee Common. There are a number of steep inclines along this walk, and so a fair degree of stamina is required!

THE WALK

❶ You will find a rough drive just to the left of the village school. Go along this to a kissing-gate, then downhill across Lee Manor Park towards the lowest point. Walking anticlockwise around the rim of an overgrown pit, aim for a stile and gate in a corner (not those under electricity wires) and join a track under trees along the bottom of the valley. To avoid mud some walkers take an easier option in the form of a parallel meandering path on the right. They eventually rejoin the track before meeting the road at the far end.

❷ Turn right on the road, and when this soon curves left and runs uphill cross a stile on the right by a pole-mounted transformer. Go uphill across a field to another stile (190°), not following the overhead wires but aiming at the left-hand extremity of the trees. Initially passing between allotments and the trees turn right at a crossing *within* the allotments (the trees will remain on your immediate right); then go through a pedestrian gate and turn left onto a rough drive. Stay with the drive (between houses) to a T-junction and kissing-gate; but before proceeding further have a look at the nice terrace of cottages opposite the chapel along to the right. For the Pheasant turn left at the T-junction. The pub is 100 yards along the drive.

❸ From the kissing-gate cross the grass and walk around the perimeter fence of a cricket ground, aiming at a very fine roof-scape of 'farm' buildings beyond the far left-hand corner. Don't go through either of the metal gates there but turn right to a field corner (beyond a small uncultivated area) and walk the field's left-hand edge to the next corner. Turn left into the next field and soon arrive at another corner. Turning right here, follow the hedge for 100 yards or so to a stile on the left – where the field edge begins to curve right.

❹ Having passed through to the adjacent field turn right and follow its right-hand edge (and the overhead wires) to a corner. Turning left out of the corner (ignore the farm gate there) stay with the right-hand hedge as far as a shallow dip in the field. Cross the stile at that point and enter yet another field at yet another corner!

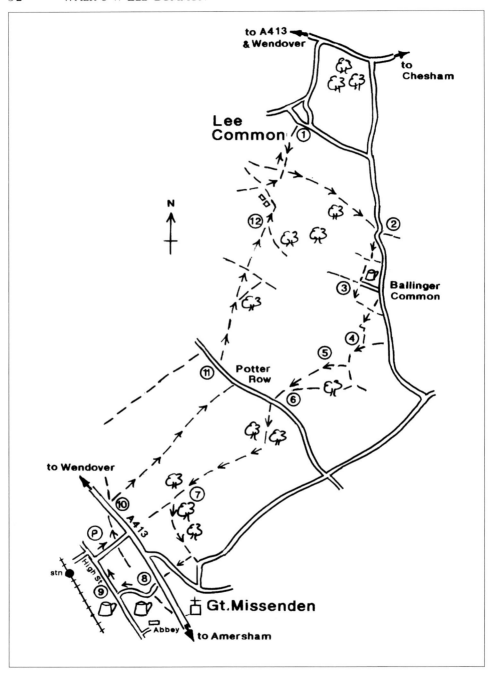

Following the left-hand hedge, pass under electricity wires and bear left with the field-edge. As a check on your position there should be sizeable wood in view beyond the left-hand field!

❺ When the hedge turns sharp but briefly left, strike forward across the field, aiming for a distant stile in a corner (240°). Many walkers have taken an easier option here, by simply following the left-hand field-edge. From the stile go through to the adjacent field and continue straight on (in your previous direction) to a stile and gate at a roadside.

❻ Cross the road to a field and aim for the mid-point of a wood on the far side. As you follow the path through the wood you may notice a series of shallow earthworks. These are the remnants of a manor which stood here in medieval times. On leaving the wood from the far side you should bear right slightly to pass between two fields and the mid-point of two pylons (250°). From the next stile go downhill along a dip, soon passing to the left of a wood.

❼ Crossing a pair of stiles lower down in the field corner, enter the left-hand wood and take the right-hand branching path immediately. Follow this meandering path uphill through the trees (with a field in view a few yards to the right) and join a narrow, level, path from the far end. On joining a drive keep forward for about 20 yards only, turning right beyond a stable block and descending a steep metalled path all the way down to Great Missenden.

❽ Passing a school and Abbey Farmhouse go forward along Church Street to the T-junction at the far end. The entrance to Missenden Abbey can be found by turning left at the T-junction. Founded in 1133 as an Augustine monastery, it is now an abbey in name only, functioning as a training and conference centre and providing a wide range of leisure courses. It also has an excellent garden nursery – worth visiting for that alone! And in the same direction you will find the Waggon and Horses pub.

❾ To continue on the walk turn right into the High Street (if coming out of Church Street) and go as far as the library, passing or entering other pubs or the tea room en route! Turn right just beyond the library and left through a metal kissing-gate (signposted 'South Bucks Way') opposite a children's play area; then walk a succession of fields straight on to the A413.

❿ Cross the A413 to a stile by a roundabout sign and follow a wide grassy track uphill (not half-left across a field), soon accompanied by a long grassy bank that is ablaze with flowers in summer – a marvellous sight! The next but one stile takes you under a complex of wires and up into a field along its dip; and a dense line of trees soon runs parallel on the right. From a kissing-gate in the far right-hand corner continue uphill, but now between a metal fence and the trees, eventually joining a metalled drive. Go forward along the drive and turn left at the road, near Park Farm, Potter Row.

⓫ The point of departure from the road is beyond a tennis court and adjacent to an old well (which extends to a depth of around 230 feet!). If you venture a little further along the road you will see what was once the Lamb public house, with its name retained on a wall. Go through a wide gap by the well and cross a large field half-left (20°), aiming at the right-hand end of a line of conifer trees. After passing the trees continue straight on, crossing a succession of three more fields. On the way you will skim an electricity pole in mid-field, go over a crossing-path, and, in the final field, descend to a dip while following a left-hand hedge. All being well you should find yourself in a small uncultivated area – where there's a very welcome seat!

⑫ Continue forward from the seat, along a track that soon curves left and passes Field End Grange and a cottage. Keep forward to a crossing in a dip, turning right there into another track. After 200 yards bear left with the track through a gap in the trees. Ignoring a branch on the right, very soon arrive at a stile and gate. These are under an electricity pole and give access to Lee Manor Park. Passing the overgrown pit on the right, ascend the park towards a pole-mounted transformer at the top. Go through the kissing-gate up there to join the drive again and return to the village.

FLAUNDEN

Length: 6½ miles

Getting there: Flaunden is not the easiest village to find, but can be approached from Kings Langley along a route that includes Chipperfield and Belsize. Kings Langley is on the A4251 and is 1 mile north of junction 20 of the M25.

Parking: In addition to roadside parking, there is a further option close to the village crossroads – in a layby in Birch Lane. The Green Dragon public house has a car park for customers.

Map: OS Landranger 166 Luton, Hertford and surrounding area (GR 017008).

Perhaps Flaunden's chief claim to fame is that the parish church was the first to be designed by Sir George Gilbert Scott, whose work included St Pancras Station Hotel and the Albert Memorial in London. For me the highlights of this village are in its heritage of lovely flint and brick cottages, and the historic associations in which they are enshrined.

Flaunden, Latimer, Chenies: a trio of lovely villages linked by a route that enjoys fine woodland, outstanding views and two crossings of the river Chess. The beauty of the river can be appreciated at the ford

---

FOOD and DRINK

The Green Dragon at Flaunden is a fine old pub, well known to walkers. It offers a very wide choice of food from sandwiches and ploughman's to 'lite bites' and 'dragon fillers' (main meals) and an interesting selection of pasta dishes. Telephone: 01442 832269. The Bricklayers Arms is ¼ mile from the village crossroads in the Bovingdon direction. There are two pubs along the walk at Chenies – the Bedford Arms (telephone: 01923 283301) and the Red Lion (telephone: 01923 282722). The Red Lion takes pride in its Chenies Lamb Pie and its rabbit and prune pie – as well as offering lighter fare. The small shop at Mill Farm, Chenies Bottom (also on the walk) is open every day (not 1-2 pm) for ice cream, yoghurts and biscuits.

---

below Mount Wood – an ideal place to rest a while before heading back to Flaunden. There are three moderate ascents along this walk: two at Latimer, one on leaving the ford.

THE WALK

❶ From the crossroads at the village centre go past the phone box and the Green Dragon and turn left into a no through road by the church. This becomes a rough drive and eventually divides by an observatory – which is used by the South-West Herts Astronomical Society. Take the right-hand branch here (a track now) and stay with it through three bends. Ignore a narrow bridleway leaving from the third bend and continue along the track to a crossing at the very end, just before the trees. Having arrived at the crossing I should now tell you that you have just walked what is locally referred to as a 'manorial coffin road'! This route apparently linked the present village of Flaunden to the old village and its church in the Chess valley. Except for a small mound and a tomb, there is nothing left on the ground from the old village.

❷ Branch half-right at the crossing and, passing between the trees and a field, follow another track until you meet a low fence, beyond which is a private bridleway. Keep right here, under the trees, then forward for a further 50 yards. Take the downhill left-hand branch at this point and soon emerge into the open. Go left and downhill again, between fields and joining a road at the bottom. Turn left at the road and soon enter the village of Latimer, where, on the green, you will find an old well and an interesting memorial to a horse!

❸ Branch right in the village and go uphill along the road almost as far as the Latimer House entrance. Leave the road there by turning left into a drive and follow this along and down to the river Chess, enjoying a marvellous view of the widened river as you go. Latimer House stands up on the hill to your right – in all its Victorian Gothic glory. Before becoming a management training centre in 1988 the house had served part of its time as the Joint Services Staff College. During World War II it was used as an interrogation centre for high ranking prisoners of war. Don't cross the river but go left over a stile just before the bridge. Follow the river – with a fence on the right – as far as a stand of tall oak trees, then bear slightly left across the grass to a stile and the road. There is a large green console near the stile, and Latimer village is now over to the left.

❹ Turn right at the road and follow this over the Chess to a road junction. Cross to a short flight of steps and a stile adjacent to

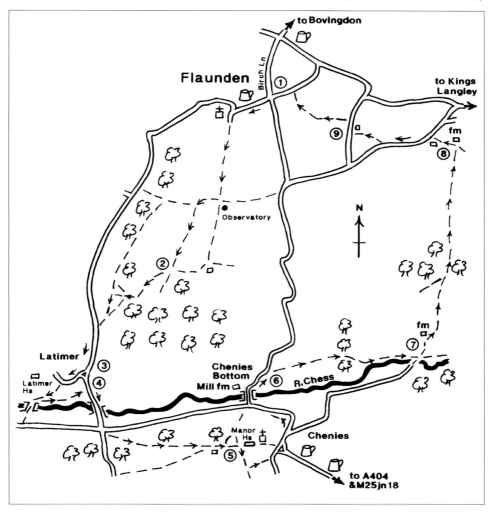

Stony Lane and climb a field half-left (110°) to a gap in the trees. Once over a stile at the right-hand side of the gap turn left to follow an almost level field-edge, with a fence and trees on the left. Stay with the trees as they evolve into woodland; and when this in turn gives way to open fields, keep forward roughly in the direction of the hilltop house. After the second of two stiles you will be up there beside the house on a wide, level track. Ignore all stiles giving access to a wood and follow the track to a metal gate and the precincts of Chenies Manor.

❺ The Manor House dates in part to the 1400s and was owned by the Earls and Dukes of Bedford for more than 400 years.

Chenies.

Later additions included a number of Tudor-style, mostly ornate, chimneys, 23 of which survive. The house and its attractive gardens are open to the public on Wednesday and Thursday afternoons from April to October. Turn right here into a wide rough drive and left at a junction in the drive, with the manor house (and a 1,000-year-old oak tree!) over to your left as you go. On entering Chenies you could continue forward through the village to the Bedford Arms or the Red Lion. Otherwise turn left; and with the village pump over to your right (which still supplies water!) go along the road to a terraced path on the left beyond the last house, Whitehill Cottage. Stay with this path all the way down to the

end, rejoining the road and continuing downhill to the first junction. Turning right at the junction you will soon encounter Dodd's Mill and, after that, Mill Farm and its farm shop. The mill, one of nine that existed on the Chess in earlier days, is now a private house. Although one of its two wheels has been retained and can be driven, it has no useful function.

❻ Having crossed the Chess and passed the farm shop leave the road at the next left-hand bend and go over a stile on the right. This places you on the terraced edge of a meadow which you should follow more or less straight on. Keep forward across the next two meadows – and over the intervening stiles – and forward again under trees. Emerging from the trees, follow a fenced path near the field-edge and soon walk parallel to the river, eventually to a ford – one of the most delightful fords anywhere!

❼ When you can tear yourself away from this lovely place take the left-hand branch of a metalled drive (at its hairpin turn) and head up towards a farm. Branch half-right to a metal gate just before the farmyard and walk the path between farm buildings and a field. After crossing the end point of a farm track where three fields meet, continue forward and uphill between fields and trees. A good woodland path takes over and eventually places you in the open near the top of the hill. Having taken you straight on it passes under power lines and meets a T-junction by Rosehall Farm.

❽ Turn left at the T-junction into a concrete drive and keep straight on along a grassy path when the drive runs into the farm. A stile leads you forward between hedges to another stile by Great Bragman's Farm. Keeping more or less straight on again, cross a meadow to a stile in the opposite corner, passing to the right of the farm as you go. Turn half-left into a lane and go along this for about 250 yards to a short flight of steps and a stile on the right. Cross the field here half-left (assuming your back is to the stile) aiming slightly left of an electricity pole and meeting a hedge corner on the far side. On arrival keep more or less straight on by following the hedge to a lane.

❾ Turn right at the lane and left into a footpath after only 70 yards – soon after passing New House Farm. After following a level path between fields to a stile, go half-right to the far right-hand corner of a large field. A stile will place you in the next field. Walk along its left-hand edge to the road at Flaunden and turn left for the village centre. As you go over the crossing en route to the Green Dragon, notice again the red telephone box. This, along with the church, is on the List of Buildings of Special Architectural or Historic Interest!

BLEDLOW

Length: 6 miles

Getting there: Bledlow can be approached from the B4009 along West Lane, midway between Princes Risborough and Chinnor, and from the A4010, turning off 1 mile south of Princes Risborough.

Parking: There is limited roadside parking in the village, and a small off-the-road parking area near the telephone box. Customers at the Lions may wish to leave their cars in the pub's own car park.

Maps: OS Explorer 2 Chiltern Hills North or Landranger 165 Aylesbury and Leighton Buzzard area (GR 778022).

Beautifully sited between the Upper and Lower Icknield Ways and overlooked by the steep beech-clad slopes of the Chiltern escarpment, Bledlow is without question the perfect English village – except that it has no shop! The Lyde Garden alongside the church is a bonus. Here the Lyde Brook issues from below the chalk and flows into a lovely landscaped ravine.

The walk climbs steeply to join the Ridgeway Trail below Bledlow Great Wood and follows it along the ridge of Lodge Hill. Much favoured by birds, butterflies and wild flowers, Lodge Hill is a jewel among hills. On returning to lower levels, the walk completes the circuit by way of two

---

FOOD and DRINK

Bledlow's one and only pub, the Lions, enjoys great popularity, and justly so. An impressive variety of meals is served there, including vegetarian dishes and a choice of around ten scrumptious sweets! Telephone: 01844 343345. Do, however, expect the company of many other customers on warm sunny weekends! There is a cafe at the Princes Industrial Estate a short distance off the walk at Horsenden; but don't expect to find it open outside working hours! Meals are obtainable at a number of pubs in Princes Risborough, 3 miles from Bledlow. The Whiteleaf Cross in Market Square is particularly recommended. Good lunchtime meals are served Monday to Saturday (only). Telephone: 01844 346834. A car park is situated near the parish church and another near Budgens' store.

---

delightful settlements, Saunderton and Horsenden, where there are frequent sitings of a brook and its associated ponds.

THE WALK

❶ Starting from a footpath opposite Piggotts and the village post box (which is not far from the church) pass between gardens and houses to a stile and field corner. Go straight on uphill along the left-hand edge of this and the next field, with the company of a hedge all the way and a dip in the second field. Cross the chalky Icknield Way track beyond the second field and continue forward across two more fields. In the process you will pass through a band of trees (in another dip) before climbing very steeply. Looking back, your reward is a superb view of Princes Risborough and the Whiteleaf Cross cut into the chalky hillside; also, well over to the right, the windmill at Lacey Green.

❷ On leaving that very steep field turn left from a stile and follow a fence and trees along the open hillside. This is the Ridgeway Trail, an 85 mile route from Ivinghoe Beacon in Buckinghamshire to Overton Hill in Wiltshire, which we shall be using over the next 2 miles. Go through a kissing-gate in the far left-hand corner of this area of hillside, then continue in more or less the same direction, but with a hedge on the right and a field left.

❸ Cross a road at the far end (half-left) to a kissing-gate (a common piece of furniture along the Ridgeway trail!) and walk the clear path straight on through two fields, turning right immediately from a kissing-gate beyond the second. With a hedge on your right at the start, soon go steeply uphill to the heights of Lodge Hill. Chances are you will enjoy seeing a great variety of wild flowers and their attendant butterflies as you make your way along the summit of the ridge.

❹ When you eventually approach the end of the ridge don't go over the stile ahead (not to be confused with a gate at the halfway point), but turn left and go downhill alongside a fence and through a kissing-gate. If in doubt simply take your cue from the plentiful supply of Ridgeway signs and acorn symbols – for the time being at least. Passing under a line of trees lower down, join the right-hand edge of a field and follow this all the way to a road.

❺ Cross the road to a track and stay with this as far as a house in mid-field. Pass to the right of the house and cross the field to its far right-hand corner, near a pole-mounted transformer. From a gate continue forward, but now across a golf course and following a line of trees on your right, eventually to a

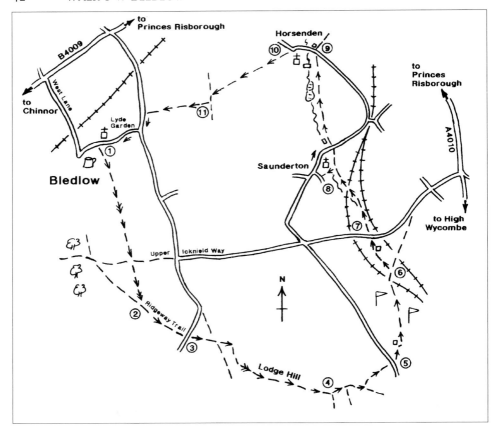

railway crossing. This is one track of the Chiltern Line from Marylebone to Princes Risborough and beyond.

❻ After crossing the track and advancing along a short path through the scrub, turn left from a kissing-gate into the lowest level of pasture. The railway now runs parallel on the left, while the Ridgeway Trail continues on its way without you. The Old Rectory, Saunderton, is ahead and a stile will lead you (surprisingly perhaps) into its garden, where you should go forward along the drive to a road.

❼ Enter a field opposite the entrance to the Old Rectory and follow a garden fence on the left. When the hedge gives way to the open field, continue forward, passing under wires and aiming for the left-hand side of a narrow neck in the field. If you see trains passing to your right as well as to your left, don't be surprised: the 'up' and 'down' lines are separated along here! After a further 200 yards go through a kissing-gate on the left and cross the railway again. On entering a field on the far side of the railway, go along the left-hand edge; likewise along the next field, but for two-thirds of its length only (you may argue that there is just one field!). Here you will find a short path (near a dual electricity pole) leading to Saunderton churchyard.

❽ Leaving the churchyard by the war memorial, go along the church path and turn right into a cul-de-sac. After enjoying the delights of Saunderton's ponds turn right at a road junction, and, after the road curves right, left into the metalled drive to Brook Cottage. A footpath signpost points the way. The drive soon runs into a path, and this in turn leads you forward across the grass and alongside a house. Continue forward through a kissing-gate and parallel to a brook on the left, then forward again through a sequence of three fields, while passing two large ponds on the left. From the far left-hand corner of the final field, turn left at the road, by the lovely thatched Gate Cottage, Horsenden.

❾ The cafe on the Princes Industrial Estate is now within range and can be reached by crossing the road and walking straight on for about 350 yards through a field and along a drive; but bear in mind that it may be closed! To continue on the walk, after turning left at the road (right if returning from the cafe) follow it as far as the church, but no further. Horsenden Manor (built in 1810) is best seen from the far side of the church, by entering the churchyard where the road turns right.

Gate Cottage, Horsenden.

⑩ To continue on the walk go into a field from a stile and gate, maintaining your previous (road) direction. Aim for a stile at the far end of the field and continue forward in the next, passing to the left of a tall pylon. A hedge and ditch will accompany you along another, longer, field, and a gap in the far right-hand corner will place you under a narrow band of trees. Turn left there and follow a path under the trees, but for 50 yards only, to a stile. Leave the trees at that point and enter the field (the first) on the right, at a corner.

⑪ Go along the left-hand edge of this and the next field and keep straight on along a drive, passing Plumtree Cottage as you go. Turn left along the road at the far end, then right into Church End, Bledlow. If you have time, do visit the Lyde Garden in Church End. You will find it most rewarding.

WALK 9

RADNAGE

Length: 3 miles

Getting there: Radnage is signposted from Chinnor Road approximately midway between Chinnor and Bledlow Ridge village; also from the A40 just ½ mile east of Stokenchurch. Both routes include narrow country lanes.	**Parking:** There is space for a few cars near St Mary's church in Radnage, where the walk starts. It is also possible to park in Horseshoe Road at the centre of the village (see sketch map).	**Maps:** OS Explorer 3 Chiltern Hills South or Landranger 165 Aylesbury and Leighton Buzzard area (GR 785979).

Overlooked by the slopes of the majestic Bledlow Ridge, this tiny village lies in a dip where narrow lanes meet. As delightful as its cottages and houses are, the village is perhaps better known for its attractive church, sited in a superb location.

The walk makes two steep sorties over the summit of Bledlow Ridge, and in so doing provides outstanding views to the north and south. Included in the views are the wooded slopes of Whiteleaf Hill above Princes Risborough, the incomparable Lodge Hill and the magnificent valley that runs into West Wycombe.

FOOD and DRINK

The Boot pub is along the walk at Bledlow Ridge (⅔ mile from the end of the circuit). A wide range of snacks and meals is offered, except at Sunday lunchtime when the choice is limited to sandwiches, ploughman's or a roast. Telephone: 01494 481659. The lovely old Three Horseshoes pub at Bennett End is well known to walkers, not least for the magnificent view from its garden! Good traditional pub food is served from Tuesday to Saturday. Come early if hoping for a snack lunch on Sunday (sandwiches, ploughman's or soup) – preferably by 1.15 pm before the roast lunches get under way. Note that the pub is closed completely on Mondays. Telephone: 01494 483273. Bennett End is signposted from the centre of Radnage village (see sketch map).

THE WALK

❶ With St Mary's parish church and its drive on your right, go uphill along Church Lane, which later changes to Radnage Lane. Go over a stile on the right just before Radnage Lane runs into a dip and cross a field downhill, aiming for the corner of an area of scrub in the valley bottom where the fields meet (60°; half-left if your back is to the stile). Passing to the right of a farm gate, keep forward over a stile and climb steeply uphill to the right of the scrub. While not omitting to glance back at the view, head up to a stile near the top of the hill and, once over this, step into the left-hand field. Continuing uphill, follow the right-hand field-edge all the way to the road on Bledlow Ridge.

❷ Turn right at the road and soon left into Chapel Lane, a no through road. Walk the entire length of the lane to a stile and gate and enter the field ahead; then enjoy another fine view – this time of the Saunderton valley. Included is Whiteleaf

Hill slightly to the left, with its chalk cross overlooking Princes Risborough, and Lodge Hill (a marvellous place on the Bledlow walk!) one mile in the half-left direction. You may also see the sails of Lacey Green windmill directly ahead on the opposite hilltop. The mill has been carefully restored to a fully working condition by the Chiltern Society. Going straight on downhill in this large field, aim for the right-hand side of a 'farm' at the bottom (50°) and cross a stile in the field corner. Turn left immediately in the next field and follow the hedge to a kissing-gate, then turn right onto a farm drive.

❸ The farm (which is partly residential) will be on your left as you make your way to a T-junction. Turn right at the T-junction and stay on the drive for ½ mile to the bungalow, Andorra.

❹ Turn right immediately beyond the far extremity of Andorra's garden – then prepare to walk back uphill! After initially following the garden hedge, continue in the same direction across a field, aiming for a farm gate and stile where three fields meet. Now the climb commences – alongside the left-hand hedge and trees to a stile. From the stile make your way up to the top right-hand corner of the next field, and there join a narrow path between fences. Houses have come into view and you are soon back on the road at Bledlow Ridge.

❺ Turn right at the road and left into a fenced path opposite the nearest corner of the Boot's beer garden. When adjacent to a field corner (from where there's another magnificent view) the path enters a wood

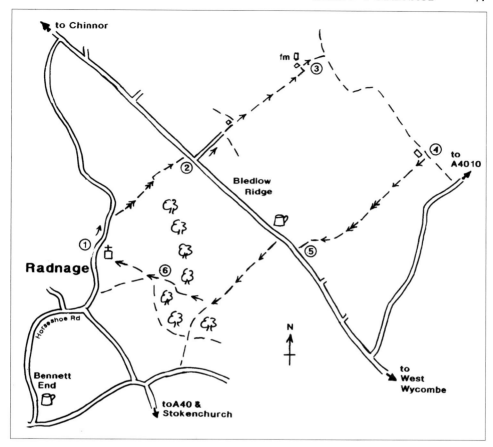

and immediately divides at a fork. Take the right-hand branch (290°), which meets a stile and dog gate after 50 yards. Thereafter the path meanders through the scrub and trees and emerges into the open. Aim for the far right-hand corner of this open scrubby area, descending the steep hillside as you go. From that corner go through a wide gap on the right and follow a fence as it curves around a wood-edge to a stile on the left – where a nearby picnic table may be just what you have been hoping for!

❻ Radnage church should now be in view – at least in part, and to end the walk there you should firstly aim for a stile in the dip of the fields. Once there bear right a little towards a stile in the opposite hedge and continue straight on to another stile in the churchyard wall. Walking the entire length of the churchyard you will arrive back at the church drive, where the walk started.

But before dashing off you really must spend at least a little of your day inside the lovely old church! The 15th-century nave roof is thought to be the finest of any

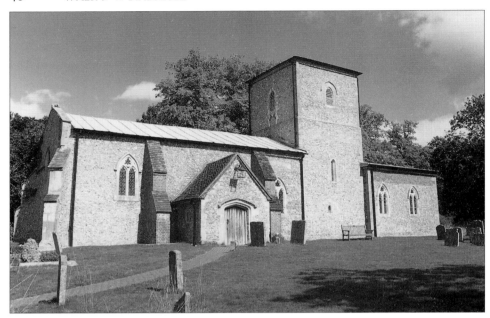

St Mary's church, Radnage.

Chiltern church. The wall paintings span no less than six centuries, and the ancient font (found in a field by a local farmer!) is considered to be Saxon. An interesting window in the chancel commemorates the Rev B.J. Corder, rector from 1904 to 1962. Numbered among his achievements is a wide range of scientific work – from cancer research to the mine detector! The perfectly sited churchyard seat also commemorates him; a memorial I greatly appreciate!

BRADENHAM

Length: 3½ miles

Getting there: Bradenham is easily found just off the A4010 some 1½ miles north-west of West Wycombe.

Parking: There is a free National Trust parking area at the top right-hand corner of the green. To reach this from the A4010 (by the Red Lion pub) go along Bradeham Woods Lane and turn first right; then soon turn left into a rough drive and follow this (carefully!) alongside the green all the way up to the parking area. There is also a small parking space near the youth hostel, opposite the churchyard.

Maps: OS Explorer 3 Chiltern Hills South or Landranger 165 Aylesbury and Leighton Buzzard area (GR 828971).

Not only is the village a Conservation Area, but many of its buildings are Listed – as of Architectural or Historic Interest. Adding to this the knowledge that much of Bradenham is in the care of the National Trust, you should be in no doubt that this particular village is not to be missed! The fine manor house – which overlooks the green from a prominent position – is of special interest in that it was the childhood home of Victorian prime minister Benjamin Disraeli. The house is now in use as a management training centre and is not normally open to the public.

FOOD and DRINK

In addition to vegetarian dishes and 'daily specials', the Red Lion pub in Bradenham serves bar meals every day. Telephone: 01494 562212. In nearby West Wycombe, the Old Plough is particularly recommended. Telephone: 01494 446648. There are also two tea rooms in West Wycombe – in the High Street and at the garden centre.

The walk offers superb views of the Saunderton valley as it follows field paths and undulates along the border of the National Trust's Park Wood. The Trust's Small Dean Farm and a lovely downland slope mark the turning point of the walk, which thereafter follows a good uphill path through the wood. Descending through a lovely wooded coombe, the walk rejoins the field paths before returning to Bradenham.

THE WALK

❶ Assuming you have parked at the top right-hand corner of the green, you should walk past the manor house gates and the church gate and cross the road to the youth hostel. If starting from the Red Lion, simply walk the length of the green to the same point. As may already be apparent, the youth hostel is housed in the former village school. It is known as the 'friendly hostel with the simple appeal'. Go along a short drive on the left side of the hostel and continue forward through a pasture, crossing two stiles as you go. Keep forward again, between fields and heading towards the left-hand edge of woodland higher up. On your approach to the wood-edge you will go over two crossings, one before you start climbing, the other by the wood-corner.

❷ Notice the interesting variety of shrubs and trees along the wood-edge as you follow this uphill from a kissing-gate; also the many wild flowers hereabouts – assuming you have arrived in the right season! When the wood-edge eventually turns left at a field corner, go downhill with it (*not* into the wood via a kissing-gate). Beyond a kissing-gate lower down, join a field-track that comes in from the left, and soon go right with this through a gap.

❸ Leave the track after 50 yards by turning right and following the wood-edge as it describes a long sweeping curve, with a field over to your left all the way. When the wood-edge eventually terminates, continue along the curve and soon pass between farm buildings. This is Small Dean Farm, a National Trust property at which much of the maintenance work of the Bradenham estate is based. The barn that overlooks the farmyard is particularly fine. If you have the opportunity to view the barn from the inside, you will see how superb are the timbers of its construction.

❹ Turn right at the road and follow this up to a National Trust parking area well beyond the farm on a lovely downland slope. Leave the road for a sunken track on the right and go straight on, ignoring a horse track that soon comes in from the left. When the track divides after a further 75 yards, keep forward along the 'No Riding Please' branch and follow this uphill through the wood, ignoring two left-hand branches and one right-hand branch as you go. White waymark arrows will guide you all the way up to the plateau at the very top.

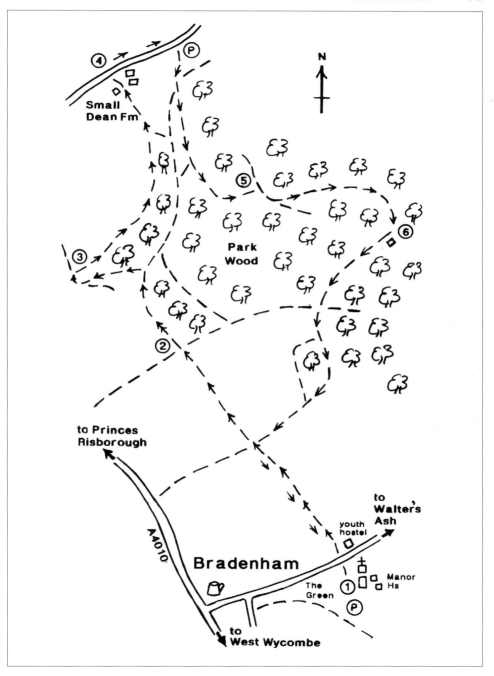

❺ On meeting the T-junction with a well-surfaced woodland drive at the top, turn right (ignoring the white arrows from now on) and follow the drive as it curves first left then right and drops down into a deep coombe.

❻ Passing a brick-built 'plant room' on the left, with houses and other buildings beyond – all part of the RAF establishment at Walter's Ash – stay on the wide drive along this very fine coombe, ignoring all

---

PLACES of INTEREST

West Wycombe is another attractive National Trust village and lies on the A40, 1½ miles to the south-east. There is much to see, including West Wycombe Manor, West Wycombe Caves and numerous historic houses.

---

branches as you go and eventually meeting a stile. After a further ¼ mile, a log seat at a crossing may jog your memory – you have passed this before! Turn left here and follow the path back to the youth hostel and the green at Bradenham.

Bradenham Manor.

LITTLE MISSENDEN

Length: 4 miles

Getting there: The village is a short distance from the A413 between Great Missenden and Amersham Old Town. It is clearly signposted from this road.	Parking: You could park along the roadside near the Crown where the walk starts or at the village centre near the church, a short distance along the walk. The Crown has a small car park for customers.	Maps: OS Explorer 2 and 3 Chiltern Hills North and South or Landranger 165 Aylesbury and Leighton Buzzard area (GR 927988).

This idyllic cottage settlement lies in the lovely Misbourne valley and is grouped around a fine manor house and an ancient church. The beauty of the church and its setting is clear to all, while its 'furniture' and wall paintings are extolled by many.

Climbing through field and woodland north of the village, the walk offers superb views of the valley through breaks in the trees. It follows a lovely woodland margin and emerges onto Hyde Heath Common – where pretty cottages, a pub and a village shop overlook the green. After leaving Hyde Heath the walk enjoys one final view of the Misbourne valley and goes over the river-bed to return to the village.

THE WALK

❶ If starting from the Crown public house or the village hall you should walk along the road (with the hall and Timber Meadow Cottages on your left at the start) to the village centre. There you will find the Red Lion pub and, beyond the crossroads, the parish church. Go over a stile into a field corner just beyond the churchyard and walk along the right-hand edge of a field as far as the A413, crossing a Misbourne footbridge as you go.

❷ Go over the A413 to a stile opposite and straight on uphill through a field, passing under power lines near the top and meeting a short fenced path by the railway – the Chiltern Line which runs from Marylebone in London to Aylesbury in Buckinghamshire. Go over the railway footbridge and soon turn left at a T-junction, by a gate. The woodland path runs uphill parallel to a field-edge and eventually meets a wide crossing-track near the summit.

❸ Turning left at the crossing (the right-hand branch leads to a gate and farm buildings), go downhill through the trees, shortly leaving the wood and entering a very scenic coombe. Cross the coombe by veering slightly left, aiming for the left-hand edge of a wood uphill on the far side. Without omitting to look back at the view, follow the edge of the wood to its first sharp corner near the summit of the fields. Turn left there from a waymark post and cross the fields for 75 yards to another wood-edge, where a track comes in from the left.

❹ With the wood-edge on your left follow the track through a sequence of two corners. Go over a stile on the left in the second corner and turn right into a path under trees. On soon leaving the trees cross a track (the one you just left!) to the stile and field opposite. Strike across the field half-left (assuming your back is to the stile), aiming a little to the right of what is a tree-clad pit (360°). Don't continue straight on from the pit (it's tempting, with a stile in view ahead!), but turn half-right and follow a fence to a stile in the far right-hand corner of this irregular-shaped field. Having crossed the stile join a straight path between fields under a narrow band of trees.

❺ Turn right into the road at the end and left at a junction after 70 yards. When the road soon turns half-left go over a stile on the right into a hedge-lined path. Go left with this then right over a stile after a few more yards. Soon enter a wood and continue to a T-junction with a rough drive. Turning right here into the drive and passing between West Lodge and another house, cross a little green to a kissing-gate.

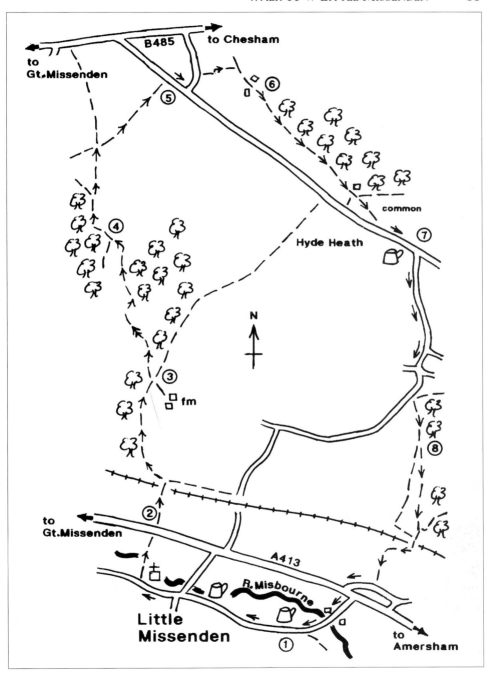

❻ You now have a long straight path just under the trees, with a field on the right all the way. Where the field eventually terminates, keep more or less forward through the wood and forward again across a green by Parson's Cottage. A footpath sign (between the house and an electricity pole) points the way, leading you to an oblique crossing and straight on to Hyde Heath Common, where there are seats to rest those flagging limbs!

❼ Leave the far end of the common by turning right into Brays Lane beyond the Plough public house; then keep forward when Brays Lane gives way to Chalk Lane. After Chalk Lane curves right go over a stile on the left at a wood corner (beyond the garden of Woodside) and branch right almost immediately into a downhill path. Having done this, there will be a field in view to the right.

❽ On leaving the wood go over a stile and enter a long field (or join the adjacent fenced path, which has the same destination). While enjoying another fine view of the Misbourne valley, make your way lengthwise across the field to a short path at the far end. Cross the railway footbridge and follow a fenced path, first right then left and down to a side road by Lime Farm. Cross the A413 to the Little Missenden turn-off and soon find yourself at the Crown public house, from where it's a short walk along the road to the village centre.

Hyde Heath Common.

WATLINGTON

Length: 6½ miles

Getting there: Watlington is on the B4009 and will be found 3 miles south-west of Lewknor and junction 6 of the M40.

Parking: There is a public car park off Hill Road (Christmas Common direction) close to the centre of the

village. Roadside parking is possible on the B4009 (Shirburn Street) a short distance in the Lewknor direction. The National Trust car park on Watlington Hill is an alternative starting point for the walk. This can be found off Hill Road 1¼ miles from Watlington (see point 5).

Maps: OS Explorer 3 Chiltern Hills South or Landranger 175 Reading, Windsor and surrounding area (GR 690945).

Situated on the historic Lower Icknield Way near the foot of the Chiltern Hills, this lively village has an attractive High Street overlooked by a fine 17th-century town hall. Beyond the High Street there are further delights – residential streets and pathways where it is a pleasure to walk. As villages go Watlington has a surprising number of useful shops, which doubtless contributes to its popularity and friendliness.

Watlington Hill – and the magnificent

FOOD and DRINK

The Carriers Arms in Hill Road (near the car park) is well liked for its good home cooking and value for money. Telephone: 01491 613470. The Fox and Hounds in Shirburn Street serves snacks and main meals, and specialises in chilli dishes.Telephone: 01491 612142. The Chequers pub is on the north side of Watlington near the end of the walk. As a change from pubs you could try the Community Shop tea room in the High Street (open Monday to Saturday as and when staffing is available) or the fish and chip takeaway in Couching Street!

---

views that it affords – is the reward that follows a steady but invigorating one-mile ascent. The steep descent includes a close pass of Watlington White Mark, a chalk hill-figure, while the concluding half mile enjoys something of Watlington's backways. The route takes the form of an unsymmetrical figure of eight; so as you walk the circuit don't be too surprised when you find yourself treading part of it twice over!

THE WALK

❶ Starting from the Old Town Hall (an island building at the main village crossroads), go along Couching Street (B4009) towards the petrol station and T-junction, noting (on the left) what was once the 'Tallow Chandler' shop. Turn left at the junction into the B480, and when this soon turns right keep forward into Spring Lane, a 'no entry' road. When this turns left keep forward again, but now on a wide gravel path between houses. Stay on the main path (not the branch bearing right beyond the houses) and follow its right-hand curve until it joins an avenue of elder trees (worth a visit in the wine-

making season!). After walking the length of the avenue turn right through a gap and go along a left-hand field-edge to a road.

❷ Turn right at the road and left to a footpath after a few yards. As you cross the field (at right-angles to the road) you should be enjoying an impressive view of the Chiltern escarpment, with Watlington Park making an appearance through a gap in the trees. On reaching the far side of the field turn left at a T-junction and walk a long straight path between fences and fields. Turn right with the path at the far end, and, following a hedge on your left, soon reach a concrete hardstanding. The drive beyond this runs into Lys Mill (for information only!). Leave the hardstanding by entering a field on the left, at a corner, then walk the entire length of the field, with a hedge on your right and the drive beyond that. (If the field is wet, you might decide that the drive is a better option!)

❸ From a stile in the field's far corner, keep forward over a five-way junction, but for a few yards only, and turn left to join a left-hand field-edge. This is a 'permissive' alternative for part of the Ridgeway Trail, which, as a metalled drive, runs parallel on the left (you could use it if you wish). Leave the field from its far left-hand corner and turn right onto the B480. Walk along the road (or better still – its grass verge) for 250 yards and turn half-left into a wide rough drive, which is signposted as a footpath.

❹ Branch left from the drive after only 60 yards – just beyond a bungalow and through a wide grassy gap. This soon evolves into a path under trees and marks the start of a

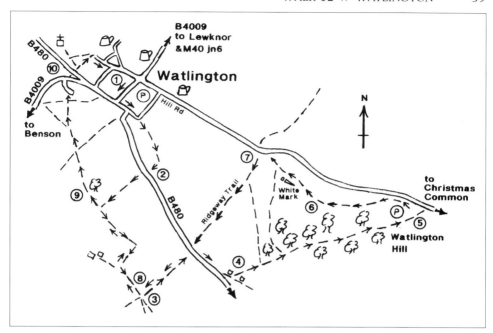

one-mile steady climb to the summit of Watlington Hill. You should keep straight on along the main path, ignoring all branches as you go.

❺ On arrival at the top turn left onto a National Trust car park and cross this to a gap opposite, with the car park entrance and a road in view to your right. From the gap (which is crossed by a bricked drainage channel) walk the length of a rectangular green and make your exit from its far right-hand corner. Descend a short flight of steps to the road and follow this downhill for 100 yards to a kissing-gate, making use of a 'sidewalk' in the process. The gate introduces a fine stretch of National Trust downland with some quite amazing views in prospect. You should keep forward across this, aiming for the highest point of the

open area while traversing the slope of the hill (260°).

❻ Go through a gap in the scrub directly ahead; and after Watlington comes into view (also directly ahead), bear right a little (330°) in order to take the least steep descent. All being well this piece of navigation will take you downhill to the tip of Watlington's White Mark, a long hill-figure that exposes the chalky hillside. The figure was cut in 1764 and has been likened to the 'ghostly shadow of a church spire lying along the hill'. The effect is best seen from the road lower down. Follow the Mark downhill and continue down on one of two paths, finally joining the Watlington road near the bottom.

❼ Leave the road after only a few yards by

turning left into the Ridgeway Trail prior to the house numbered 90. After ½ mile of the trail cross the next road (also destined for Watlington) to a field-side path opposite, which you may recognise from earlier in the walk. Follow the field-edge straight on, with a hedge on the right, all the way to the end.

❽ Turn right from the field-end and cross a five-way junction to a stile and field-corner. Walk the left-hand edge to the far corner and turn right onto a hardstanding, after which follow a path between hedge and field, soon turning left with it between fences. Although you are walking the outward route in reverse, this coincidence soon terminates; instead of turning right out of the fenced path keep straight on towards a knot of trees.

❾ Passing to the left of the trees and following a stream-bed thereafter, go over a crossing-track (briefly right, then left) and keep forward for 150 yards to a field-corner on the right. Leave what is now a farm track by turning half-right into a waymarked path on the right. This runs between a hedge and the triangular-shaped field to a T-junction at the far right-hand corner. Turn right there to a kissing-gate and left immediately in a field; then follow the field's left-hand edge to a corner. After passing briefly between houses turn left into a metalled drive (The Goggs) then right into a road at a T-junction.

Chapel Street, Watlington.

⑩ Cross the road after 25 yards and join a metalled path between the houses numbered 12 and 14. Soon cross another road and keep straight on between gardens (along another metalled path), ignoring a left-hand branch as you go. You will eventually meet Mansle Garden, a triangular green (with seats for tired walkers!) and Church Close soon after that. For the Chequers pub go left at the next turning, then left again; for the High Street keep straight on. Before walking the High Street do take a view of Chapel Street – a left turn from the war memorial.

FINGEST

Length: 3 miles

Getting there: Fingest can be approached from the A40, signposted 1½ miles west of West Wycombe, and from the B482 1 mile west of Lane End.	Parking: This is possible by the church or, for customers, at the Chequers pub. You may find it easier to park at Turville, and start the walk there (see point 7).	Maps: OS Explorer 3 Chiltern Hills South or Landranger 175 Reading, Windsor and surrounding area (GR 777911).

If you do not already know Fingest, you have a pleasure and a delight in store! The beautiful church, with its unusual twin-gabled tower, overlooks a meeting of country ways. Here there are some lovely old dwellings, humble and grand, and the historic Chequers inn.

From Fingest you have the prospect of a long gradual ascent in the direction of Cadmore End. Doubling back through Hanger Wood there follows a roller-coaster of hills (twice steeply down, once steeply up), with magnificent views. After an interlude at Turville – that most beautiful of Chiltern villages – your walk concludes with a ½ mile amble back to Fingest.

FOOD and DRINK

There are two pubs along the walk – the Chequers at Fingest (telephone: 01491 638335) and the Bull and Butcher at Turville (telephone: 01491 638283). The Chequers offers a wide choice of bar food, including vegetarian meals. Especially recommended is the home-made chicken and game pie. But be warned – there are no chips! The lovely village of Skirmett (not on the walk) has two pubs also. It is ½ mile south of Fingest and worth visiting for its own sake. Simple refreshments (tea, coffee, cold drinks and ice cream) are available during the summer at Cadmore End's little garden nursery. This requires a short diversion from the walk.

THE WALK

❶ From the T-junction near Fingest church, go along Chequers Lane to a footpath on the right beyond Church Cottage. Although this takes you between gardens to a stile, don't go over the stile (it leads into a field) but take the fenced path *between* fields. From a stile at the end of this path continue forward, but now along a terraced field-edge and following overhead wires. At the next stile where the field-edge curves left, a track comes in from the right. Go forward along this, still following the wires and climbing gradually uphill.

❷ Further uphill near a group of sheds, the track divides two ways. Take the left-hand branch and continue uphill (the other is more or less level). It's now a simple matter of keeping forward along the track under the trees for ¾ mile, ignoring all crossings and branches (especially a half-left gated branch from the first summit in the track) until you see a stile and gate on the left and a board proclaiming 'No Bikes, Church Path'. Here the track emerges into the open and describes an S-bend.

❸ Although the stile and gate marks your return path (a sharp hairpin turn) you may wish to divert to Cadmore End before joining it. There is a good view to be enjoyed along this short diversion, and, on arrival, a delightful little garden nursery that in summer serves hot and cold drinks and ice cream. With its collection of pet animals, the nursery also provides good entertainment for children. For the diversion, keep forward on the track for ¼ mile, ignoring a branch on the left as you go. This will make your total distance 3½ miles, instead of 3. To continue on the walk from the nursery: retrace your steps along the track through an S-bend to where the track passes under trees. Branch right here into Church Path (a left hairpin turn if you didn't divert to Cadmore End) and follow this uphill through the wood for just under ¼ mile to a crossing-track.

❹ Now take care – go over the crossing-track and continue forward for 25 yards only, to where the path recommences its climb. If you see a multiplicity of signs here, and boards giving the history of the woodland, you are in the right place! Turn right here into the path signposted to Chequers Lane and soon find a pair of seats on a summit level in the woodland. Turn half-left now, following the waymarks along a wide grassy path and soon descending steeply through the wood. When the path divides lower down (after about 100 yards) keep straight on towards a clearing – beyond which the fields are in view. Enter the nearest field from a stile and go steeply down to the road at the bottom, enjoying a superb view of Fingest and the Hambleden Valley as you go.

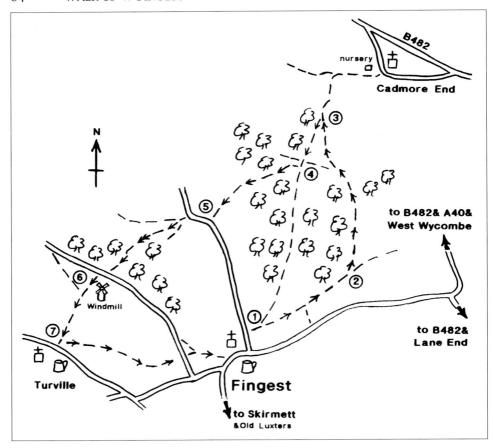

❺ Turn right at the road and leave this for a gap on the left after 75 yards. Go along the bridleway here and soon enter a field from a stile (not into the wood on the left), allowing the bridleway to continue without you. Climbing the gentle slope of the field straight on, aim for a gap in the wood-edge ahead (250°), and once there continue uphill through the wood. There's a stile and a twist in the path on the way up, followed by a sighting of a house at the top.

❻ Just beyond the house is Ibstone Mill, a well-known landmark. Built in the mid-1800s, this smock mill was derelict and fire-damaged in the 1970s, but later rebuilt. Although it makes a very pretty picture, the mill no longer functions as such, and the sails are purely ornamental. Turn right along the road here and left soon after passing the entrance gates to the house. There now follows a very steep descent of the open hillside towards Turville, but if you circle well over to the right (as far as a stile and its associated footpath) rather than going straight on down between a

PLACES of INTEREST

Old Luxters Vineyard and Brewery makes an interesting excursion with which to end the day. Signposted from the Hambleden road 1½ miles south of Fingest, Old Luxtors lies at the top of a long and very steep road. It is open daily until 6 pm (5 pm in winter) and admission is free.

fence and the trees, you will find the going a little easier. On meeting the fence later on, continue down, over stiles and into Turville village.

❼ It is not necessary for me to extol the beauty of this unspoilt Chiltern village; it is plain for all to see! Much of Turville's history is vested in the church. This is equally so to the present day: the village and its church provide the setting for the television series *The Vicar of Dibley*! Retracing your steps from the village (starting near the Old School House) soon go over a stile and enter the right-hand field from a gate. Follow a garden fence for just a few yards and then veer slightly left and uphill towards the left side of a knot of trees (100°). This places you on a level, shady path (a marvellous place for flowers and butterflies in summer!) and in turn leads to a road. By crossing the road and bearing right at a junction of paths, you are soon back in Fingest.

Turville.

PENN

Length: 4½ miles

Getting there: Penn is on the B474 between Beaconsfield and Hazlemere, near High Wycombe. The starting point for the walk is opposite the green (Tylers Green) and its large pond.	Parking: There is a small public parking space near the Red Lion pub at the start of the walk and another in Elm Road nearby, opposite what was once the butcher's shop. Roadside parking is possible alongside the green, but not on the B474.	Maps: OS Explorer 3 Chiltern Hills South or Landranger 175 Reading, Windsor and surrounding area (GR 907937).

Elm Road, an attractive side road at Penn, together with the green and its pond, compensates to a large extent for the traffic which passes through the village along the B474. As it happens, we have to thank this road for the few shops that remain, both here and at nearby Tylers Green. One of these is a second-hand bookshop – worth coming to Penn for that alone!

This walk alternates between woodland and open fields through attractively undulating countryside. There are fine

FOOD and DRINK

The Red Lion at Penn, where the walk starts, has a good choice of ales and a wide-ranging menu. It is well known for its ploughman's, salads and steaks, also for its Prawn Special. Telephone: 01494 813107. The Crown is situated at the mid-point of the walk. This is a Chef and Brewer pub with food available 'all day, every day'. The snacks menu includes sandwiches, jacket potatoes and cream teas. Telephone: 01494 812640. The Royal Standard of England, (telephone: 01494 673382), is at Forty Green along the walk while the Horse and Groom (Telephone: 01494 812229) is a little off the walk at Tylers Green.

views along all points of the compass, views which include the Surrey hills. The historic church of the Holy Trinity, Penn, is encountered en route, as well as a delightful cottage settlement near the end. With Penn being at a high point of the Chilterns, the walk includes two steady, but not too demanding, ascents.

THE WALK

❶ Go along the rough drive to the left of the Red Lion pub (which is opposite the pond) and follow this straight on. Coleshill windmill comes into view directly ahead on the distant horizon as you approach Puttenham Place Farm. Leave the drive when it runs into the farm and keep forward along a footpath, with a garden hedge on your left.

❷ Pass through the gap ahead when you are adjacent to the last of the buildings and turn left along a field-edge. Soon turn right out of the field corner (at a junction of paths) and stay with the field-edge, resuming your previous direction. With Penn's church in view uphill on your right and Penn Bottom running parallel below,

continue forward along the next field-edge – which eventually coincides with a wood-edge.

❸ Where another path crosses the field from the right, and 50 yards before the wood-edge curves half-right, turn left and enter the wood. Strictly speaking you should turn right immediately on entering the wood, but if this proves difficult you should go deeper into the wood and turn right after 20 yards (about 25 paces), then follow the waymark arrows through the wood. Passing a pit on your right, keep forward at a Y-junction after a further 10 yards (90° – the left-hand branch) and follow the waymark arrows to a gap, where once stood a stile. Leave the wood at this point and turn right to follow its outer edge, with a young conifer plantation and a fence on your left. Turn right on reaching the road at the bottom and continue past the magnificent Penn House Farm and the drive to Church Knowl.

❹ Turn right at the first road junction and soon have a view of Church Knowl, with its attractive gable-ends. The large sarsen stones by the roadside at this point were unearthed during cable laying and extension work on the house. Proceeding uphill along the lane, go over a stile on the right after ¼ mile (just before the trees) and continue uphill, but now along a left-hand field-edge. (You could alternatively stay in the lane, branching right at a Y-junction and for safety's sake re-entering the field before the lane gets very steep-sided.)

❺ Leave the field at the top corner by the Crown public house, Penn, and cross the

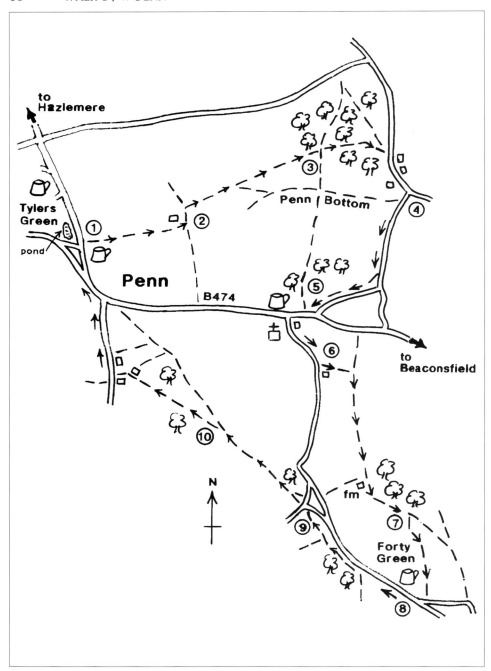

B474 (uphill a little) to Paul's Hill. The terrace of cottages along Paul's Hill are a delight – as is Holy Trinity church opposite. Notice in particular the magnificent flint tower with its rare one-handed clock and its 15th-century door. The seats in the churchyard are ideal for quiet contemplation – and for gathering strength!

❻ Descending Paul's Hill you will find a footpath just before The Vicarage – the last house on the left. From this path soon enter a field and go along its right-hand edge, with a superb view to your right – which includes the distant Surrey hills. Turn right into a metalled drive and follow this straight on, leaving it when it runs into

Underwood. Continue ahead for a few more yards along what is now a rough drive; and when this soon enters a farmyard, keep forward along a footpath just inside a wood. The path soon turns half-left and (after 150 yards) runs deeper into the wood. Now don't go dashing on, but look for a short waymarked path on the right leading to a stile and giving access to the sharp right-hand corner of a field.

❼ Your next port of call is a hedge corner in the direction half-left (assuming your back is to the stile) across the field (160°). On arrival at the corner keep to the upper edge of the sloping field, with the hedge now on your right. From the far right-corner of the field go along a narrow path

Cottages on Paul's Hill seen from the churchyard at Penn.

between hedges and join a rough drive by the Royal Standard of England. Turn right into the drive and right again into a lane, by the pub's car park.

❽ Follow the lane downhill and go over a stile on the left at the lowest point. On entering the wood here, turn right immediately and walk parallel to the road (do not take the other path running steeply uphill through the wood). After 90 yards the path starts to climb and moves away from the road. When you reach the upper wood-edge near the top of the hill, don't go into the field there but turn right, staying just within the wood. With the field-edge close by on the left, the path climbs gradually, eventually meeting a lane.

❾ Turn left into the lane and soon cross to a bridleway opposite, at a road junction. Keeping a field in view to your left, continue through the wood, finally emerging under a narrow band of trees. Now take care – after a further ¼ mile, and at a field boundary, go over a stile on the left and enter a field at its corner.

❿ Cross the field by aiming at a dip in the tree-line at the top. This is slightly left (310°) with respect to your previous direction along the bridleway. Look back at the view as you cross the stile up there, then continue forward across a meadow to another stile. Soon join a drive near the houses and turn right into a road by Thae Cottage, following this to the B474. Turn left for the green, where the walk started.

CHALFONT ST GILES

Length: 7 miles

Getting there: Chalfont St Giles is just off the A413 midway between Amersham and Chalfont St Peter.	Parking: There is a public car park opposite the village pond, and convenient roadside parking in Bowstridge Lane. The latter is situated off the High Street a little uphill from the parade of shops (not in the A413 direction).	Maps: OS Explorer 3 Chiltern Hills South or Landranger 176 West London area (GR 991935).

Chalfont St Giles retains all the elements of an attractive, lively village: good shops, numerous pubs, an interesting parish church, a pond and a village green. While some of us know it as the setting for a *Dad's Army* feature film (as Wilmington on Sea!), others associate it with John Milton and the cottage where he completed *Paradise Lost*.

After following the Misbourne valley for ¾ mile, the walk gently rises to the heights above Chalfont St Giles, where the view extends to the Surrey hills. It skims Seer Green before arriving at Jordans, a

---

FOOD and DRINK

Tea-Time, a tea room in the High Street, serves morning coffee, snacks, lunches and cream teas. It is open daily from 10 am (1.30 pm on Sunday) to 5.30 pm. Telephone: 01494 871099. Old Jordans Guest House (halfway along the walk) serves morning coffee, lunch (by prior arrangement) and afternoon tea (from 3 pm to 5 pm). Since there will be days when this service is not available, it is worth phoning beforehand to be certain. Telephone: 01494 874586. If you'd rather have a pub meal, you would be very happy with the White Hart at Three Households, 2½ miles into the walk. Here you can enjoy anything from a snack to a substantial meal – in a no smoking area if preferred. Telephone: 01494 872441. A similar choice is available at the Three Horseshoes in Seer Green, further along the walk. Telephone: 01494 677522. Seer Green and Jordans each have their own village shop.

---

beautiful village steeped in the history of the Quaker movement. Beyond Jordans the walk enjoys a passage through the estate land of Chalfont Grove and along the levels above the Misbourne valley.

THE WALK

❶ The walk commences along a rough drive adjacent to Up Corner (a road!) near the Crown. The drive is signposted 'South Bucks Way' and soon passes under tall trees. Where it curves left beyond the last house, keep straight on along a footpath, following a fence on the right; and when the path emerges into the open, keep forward again by some bungalows and along another rough drive to a lane. A short diversion along the lane to the right will give you sight of the bed of the river Misbourne, which you may find is dry. Due to extraction of up to 65% of the water for public supply, the Misbourne has often dried up. At the time of your visit you may well find that the river is flowing again,

thanks to a scheme to extract alternative water from the Colne and Thames valleys.

❷ Back where you were, and continuing in your previous direction, leave the lane when it soon turns left – by the entrance to The Old Mill. A track takes you forward from this point, runs between fields and narrows to a path. When it enters a wood keep forward just inside the right-hand edge. Now take care – soon after leaving the main body of the wood (25 yards and no more!) and directly opposite a corner in the right-hand fence, branch half-left into a waymarked path.

❸ Join a field from this branch after a few yards, then cross the field along its shallow dip to a stile on the opposite side (250°). The stile is in a corner but this will not be apparent until you are part-way across the field. From the stile keep straight on uphill between a fence and an interesting line of gnarled trees, with fields on each side. From a stile and gate near the top keep forward under trees and join a short drive by farm buildings.

❹ Turn right at a T-junction and soon left for 'Froghall' at a four-way signpost. A pole-mounted transformer is in sight nearby. Still climbing, and passing a wood on your right, go over a stile at the top and enter a field at its corner. After absorbing the magnificent view – which includes the Surrey hills – keep forward to a kissing-gate in the far right-hand corner and turn left into a road, at an S-bend.

❺ Descending the hill until it levels out, go over a stile on the right and cross a field

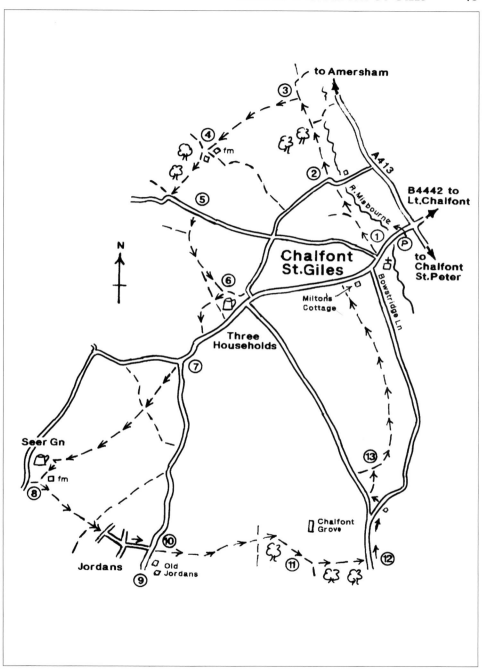

along its shallow dip at right-angles to the road (200°). Keep straight on from a stile, along a series of three left-hand field-edges, with houses and their gardens coming into view ahead. For the excellent White Hart pub at Three Households keep forward when you arrive at a footpath junction by a corner of the gardens, then turn right on meeting a road. And when you are fed and watered, come back to this point!

❻ Turn right at the corner of the gardens (left if returning from the pub) and walk behind the gardens, following the field-edge as you go. Ignore the two stiles on the left (the first is private, the second connects with a field corner) and keep forward into the next field. Don't continue to the end of the second field but turn left into yet another field and follow its left-hand edge to the road at Three Households, opposite Shearmans. Turn right in the road and stay with it to a junction, while enjoying the prospect of some fine old houses – Bowles Farm, Court and Cottage.

❼ Leave the road junction to the right of Twitchell's Lane and enter the sharp corner of a field. Initially following a garden hedge, launch yourself across the field and keep straight on through a gap at the far end. A tree-line will accompany you along part of the next field and through a recreation ground. From the far left-hand corner of the recreation ground, join a field-side path between a fence and Seer Green's gardens, and follow this all the way to a farm and beyond, ignoring three gaps on the right en route.

❽ After passing the farm and its fence you could go forward along a rough drive between brick walls to the old part of Seer Green, where you will find the Three Horseshoes pub; but to continue on the walk you should turn left into a wide path. With the farm remaining over to your left at the start (but out of sight) follow this path between fields and into a dip; then proceed uphill to the first of Jordans' houses and straight on to the village green – where you will find seats and a shop. With the green on your left, continue forward along the road to a T-junction, where a short diversion to the right will take you to Old Jordans. For safety you could use a path running parallel behind the trees.

❾ Originally a farm dating back to the early 1600s (at least) Old Jordans was in that century associated with the Society of Friends (the 'Quakers'). Well-known Quakers such as George Fox and William Penn, founder of Pennsylvania, worshipped here. The magnificent barn was part of the farm and is said to consist of timbers from the ship *Mayflower*, in which the Pilgrim Fathers sailed to America. While Old Jordans now functions as a Quaker guest house and conference centre (and more besides), what may be of interest to you at this moment is that it serves refreshments to passers-by! A short footpath links the centre's car park to the Friends Meeting House and the graveyard where William Penn and his family are buried. The house has much of interest and is well worth a separate visit – when time is not of the essence!

❿ Back at the road junction go through a kissing-gate and along the drive to Jordans

---

PLACES of INTEREST

Milton's Cottage with its attractive garden is open to the public from March to October (inclusive) on Wednesday to Sunday from 10 am to 1 pm and 2 pm to 6 pm.

Farm – straight on if coming from the green; and when the drive runs into the farm continue forward on a footpath between fences and fields. When a stile places you in a field keep straight on along the left-hand edge to another stile. This will lead you forward again, eventually to a stile and gate by a huge pylon, then onto a metalled farm drive. Cross the drive and walk the right-hand edge of a meadow – with a wood on your immediate right. Go over a stile in the far corner (not through a farm gate nearby) and enter the wood. Following the path through the wood soon leave it and enter the estate of Chalfont Grove, with its scattering of tall trees.

❶ Keep straight on across the estate towards a wood on the far side and go through a metal gate by the corner of a high security fence. The fence encloses the house and grounds of the Services Sound and Vision Corporation (SSVC), an organisation responsible for the production and transmission of radio and television programmes for service personnel worldwide. Although the property dates back many centuries, the house in its present form is largely of the late 1800s. In the 17th century, when religious dissenters were persecuted, Chalfont Grove became a secret meeting place for Quakers. When you are a short distance beyond the gate (20 yards) you have a choice between following the security fence all the way to a road or branching right along a much more pleasant 'permissive' path through the wood. If you choose the latter you must be sure to branch left when in sight of a road 80 yards ahead and rejoin the security fence at its next corner.

❷ Turn left at the road here and branch right into Bowstridge Lane after ¼ mile, having passed the entrance gate to the SSVC centre. Leave the lane after only 100 yards and join a path opposite Grove Cottage. On meeting the main road again leave it immediately by turning right into another (hedged) path; and when this terminates at a T-junction (with a fence and field ahead) turn right again.

❸ Your task now is to keep straight on for one mile all the way back to Chalfont St Giles. This takes you alongside an old cherry orchard, in and out of a dip, through a recreation ground and alongside a school. Ignore all branches and roads in the process and eventually go downhill to the village. On arrival, turn right for Milton's Cottage and the High Street.

EWELME

Length: 4½ miles

Getting there: Ewelme is signposted (1 mile) from the B4009 midway between Watlington and Benson; also from the Crowmarsh roundabout on the A4130 1 mile east of Wallingford.	Parking: This is possible on the road above the church, either alongside the churchyard or by the Old Rectory. The walk starts from this road. There is a small car park near the cricket field a short distance along the walk.	Maps: OS Explorer 3 Chiltern Hills South or Landranger 175 Reading, Windsor and surrounding area (GR 647915).

Certainly one of the loveliest villages in all Oxfordshire, Ewelme is also endowed with rich architectural, historic and human interest. The church, the cloister and the school are of one entity, each part linked physically and spiritually to the others. Almost unchanged since the day it was built, the 15th-century church has much to interest the historian, including a close association with the descendants of Geoffrey Chaucer, the poet. The school is thought to date from 1450, and claims to be the oldest church school to be incorporated in the state system while using its original building. The cloister is surrounded by 13 almshouses, founded in 1437. Visitors are welcome to enter the cloister, but are asked to respect the privacy of the residents.

Perhaps the most striking feature of the walk is the contrast between the oasis that is Ewelme and the wide open spaces of the surrounding countryside. On leaving the village the walk crosses the lovely Cow Common and skirts the lower slopes of Ewelme Downs. It enjoys views of the magnificent sweep of Swyncombe Downs before returning to Ewelme along bridleways and farm tracks that seem to be 'on top of the world'. There is a real sense of isolation along this walk, but it is of an easy distance and the ascents are of a moderate kind.

THE WALK

❶ Assuming you have parked in the road above the church, take the metalled path that runs downhill alongside the church-

The almshouses at Ewelme.

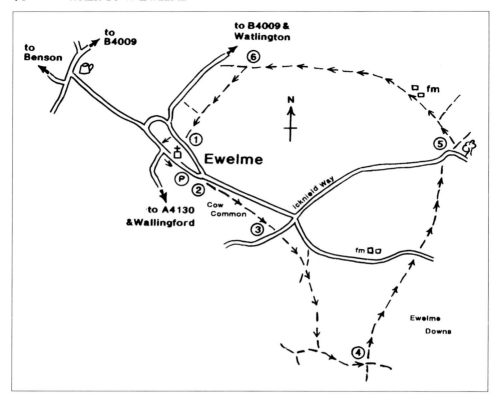

yard wall. Turn left along the road at the bottom and immediately keep forward at the road junction. After passing the school follow the road to the cricket green and car park – where you may have left your car.

❷ Cross the car park to a kissing-gate and go forward along the left-hand side of Cow Common, a very large pasture. Although the path through the pasture may not be all that clear, your objective once in it is a kissing-gate at the far end, about 150 yards from the far left-hand corner. The most frequently-used route is firstly along the left-hand edge as far as a stile (in the hedge), then quarter-right across the

pasture to the kissing-gate.

❸ From the kissing-gate cross a road to the bridleway opposite and stay with this for ¾ mile, eventually ascending the lower slope of Ewelme Downs. Turn left at a T-junction into a farm track and follow this downhill to a crossing in the dip of the fields. Ewelme Down House will be in view half-left (on the hilltop) as you descend.

❹ Turn left at the crossing and go uphill on a wide track, with the house now on the right and (quite soon) a superb view ahead of Swyncombe Downs. On meeting a metalled drive after ½ mile cross to a bridleway opposite and walk straight on along a succession of two field-edges, with a hedge on the left in the first field, and on the right in the second. Still enjoying that view, continue all the way to a road and turn right.

❺ When the road soon turns right keep straight on along a chalky track (the Icknield Way), but for 30 yards only, to a beechwood corner. Turn left here into a wide farm track between fields and stay with it past Huntingland Farm; then, after a further ½ mile, continue forward on what becomes a grassy bridleway. The cooling towers at Didcot will be in view directly ahead, distantly, also the two peaks of the Sinodun Hills. Walk along the grassy bridleway for about ⅓ mile to a stile on the left.

❻ Now take care! You should find the stile in a field corner (it may be damaged and overgrown) 50 yards *before* the bridleway passes under overarching hedgerows. This should not be confused with an earlier stile (of sorts!) adjacent to an oil pipeline marker. Climb the field diagonally to the nearest end of a thin line of trees situated at the top of the hill to the left of a group of houses. This is half-right if your back is to the stile (230°). Once there keep forward by following a path alongside the trees back into Ewelme.

Now do make sure you haven't missed any part of this delightful village! The best route to take is down the churchyard path to the church. From inside the church you are linked directly to the almshouses (do remember to respect the residents' privacy) and from these to the road at the bottom. Turn right along the road and walk as far as the pond and the village shop. Turn right by the pond and first right for the church, where this circumnavigation began. Stay on the road if you require the car park.

CROCKER END

Length: 3½ miles

Getting there: First find Nettlebed on the A4130 and you are almost there! Crocker End is signposted near the huge pot kiln at Nettlebed, not far from the High Street. Taking your cue from the signpost, drive straight on above the green at Nettlebed and go over an oblique crossing to Crocker End.

Parking: There is some parking space by the green at Crocker End. There is also space near the pot kiln at Nettlebed – a stone's throw from the Sun pub! Since the walk passes that way (near its conclusion), you would need to start your walk by following directions from point 8.

Maps: OS Explorer 3 Chiltern Hills South or Landranger 175 Reading, Windsor and surrounding area (GR 709868).

Who could imagine that this peaceful Chiltern retreat was once, along with Nettlebed, home to an industrious community of brick, tile and pot makers? As long ago as the early 1400s, 200,000 bricks were made here for nearby Stonor House – at a cost of £40 plus carriage! Crocker End is now a delight to the eye, and a superb starting point for some good Chiltern walks.

Much of this easy-going walk is along woodland drives, tracks and paths – ideal

---

FOOD and DRINK

The Sun is a delightful little pub on the B481, just off Nettlebed's High Street near the end of the walk. If you are 'into jugs' you will be intrigued by the 250 or so examples decorating the ceiling of the bar! Locally farmed meat and eggs are used extensively, and fresh fruit and vegetables come direct from a wholesale market. The pub is well known for its bacon butties – the ideal lunchtime snack for walkers! If hoping to lunch here at weekends you are well advised to book a table in advance. Telephone: 01491 641359. The White Hart in Nettlebed's High Street serves meals and afternoon teas daily (telephone: 01491 641245); and there is a community shop attached to the post office.

---

for one of those hot summer days when a little shade is appreciated! There are also some fine views across arable fields, and a visit to the historic village of Nettlebed, which is on the old coach road from Henley to Oxford.

THE WALK

❶ To start the walk you will need to head towards the 'closed' end of the common at Crocker End (by Lawers and the post box) and branch half-right from a Y-junction. Follow the road between houses numbered 23 and 25 and soon pass what was once the Carpenters Arms pub. Keep right at the road junction here and go in and out of a dip and through a hamlet announced as Catslip. On arriving at the A4130 cross to a bridleway opposite and continue forward along what soon becomes a good wide woodland track.

❷ After about 200 yards a series of prominent white waymark arrows will direct you half-right off the track and into a narrow path (220°). This turn-off is about 50 yards *before* the track describes an S-bend – a feature that should help to dispel any doubts! Soon go left at a T-junction and stay on the most-used path, following the white arrows over a crossing and into a dip. A track running along the dip should be ignored except for the purpose of crossing it and continuing more or less straight on uphill.

❸ You will see a large earth mound about 50 yards to your left before the path comes briefly out into the open and meets a waymarked T-junction. Turn left at the T-junction into a good wide path. This soon runs parallel with a shallow ditch and bank and, after 300 yards, meets a junction of ways. There is a pole-mounted transformer at this point, and a bungalow in view to your left. Keep forward here into a metalled drive under trees, with fields in view to your left.

❹ Pulling out of a shallow dip after 250 yards, you will arrive at a five-way crossing near Rose Tree Cottage, where Merrimoles Farm is signposted. Turn right here and stay on the metalled drive all the way to the B481.

❺ Cross the B481 to a bridleway opposite, and, after passing the entrance to Nuffield Saw Mill, keep forward on a track under trees, with a field on your immediate left. Ignore a stile on the left after 100 yards – and a path on the right soon after that – and stay on the track under a wide band of trees.

❻ Eventually entering a wood, look for a stile on the right after the bridleway has descended a little – over a distance of about 50 yards. Having crossed the stile go along

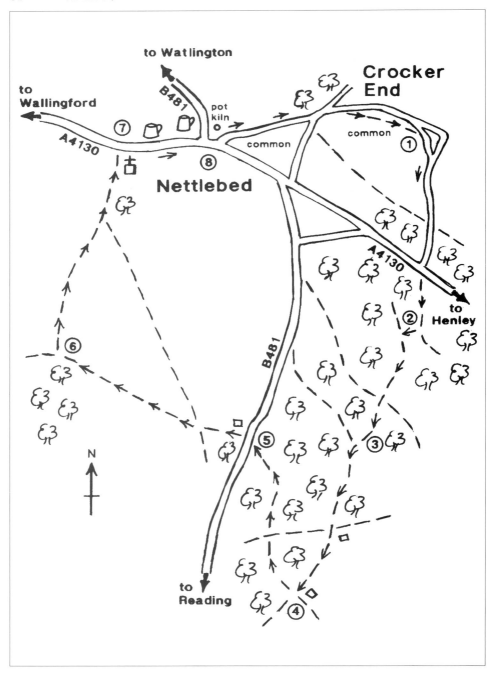

you will see the restored pot kiln, a reminder of the brick and tile industry that thrived in these parts from the Middle Ages onwards. A display panel at the base of the kiln gives more information, including the fact that this is one of five known kiln sites in the area.

the right-hand edge of a field – on a farm track and with a hedge on the right – and stay the course all the way to Nettlebed church and the High Street.

❼ Turn right along the busy High Street and left just beyond the B481 turning. Here

❽ Follow the road between Nettlebed's green and the houses (Malt House and others) and go straight on over an oblique crossing (not towards Magpies). There is no need to stay on the road thereafter: simply join a signposted path that runs the length of the green at Crocker End.

HAMBLEDEN

Length: 4 miles

Getting there: Hambleden is 1 mile north of the A4155 at Mill End, between Henley and Marlow.	Parking: Being a very popular village with visitors, roadside parking space in Hambleden is often 'all taken'. There is a public car park near the Stag and Huntsman, but the shady lane just west of the church is a good alternative on a hot summer's day!	Maps: OS Explorer 3 Chiltern Hills South or Landranger 175 Reading, Windsor and surrounding area (GR 784865).

It comes as no surprise that this quintessentially English village is a much valued Conservation Area and highly favoured by artists, film makers and photographers. Complete with its village pump, the central square is overlooked by the parish church and by attractive cottages and cottage gardens. The little Hamble Brook, which is often dry, passes through the village and links the level pastures, while up above are the towering hills of the Hambleden Valley.

What makes this walk so special are the views that can be enjoyed of the valley –

FOOD and DRINK

The Stag and Huntsman, Hambleden's one and only pub, serves home-made meals seven days a week, with choices that range from the simple to the sublime – from ploughman's lunches to chargrilled ostrich steaks! It has a very spacious garden – ideal for the popular weekend barbecues. Telephone: 01491 571227. Teas with delicious home-made cakes are available at the parish church on Sunday afternoons and bank holidays from the end of May to the end of September. The village also has a small shop – unusual in this day and age!

from the heights above Hambleden and from the lush pastures that fill the valley floor. The buildings that grace the countryside are an additional delight: Hutton's Farm on the hilltop; Colstrope Farm in the valley; the cottages at Pheasant's Hill. The walk commences with a very steep climb – after that it's plain sailing!

THE WALK

❶ From the public car park or the Stag and Huntsman turn right and go uphill along a quiet lane. Glancing over the wall on the left you will see the flint and brick manor house, in all its Jacobean splendour. When a drive goes off to the right (to Kenricks), keep straight on along what becomes a roughly surfaced lane. This rises steeply, enters a wood beyond the last house and evolves into a footpath. As you continue uphill through the wood you should ignore all turnings by staying on the main path, taking your cue from the waymark arrows and enjoying at least one superb view of the Hambleden valley.

❷ On leaving the wood keep forward along the left-hand edge of a field, and, by the second electricity pole, turn left at a crossing into a metalled drive. When the drive runs into the yard of Hutton's Farm, go forward into a short path between trees and a field. Soon cross a stile and turn left into a farm track; then branch half-right to a stile and field gate after only 30 yards. Follow this branching track alongside the field-edge and go half-right with it from the field-end (not left!).

❸ Great care is now required! After you enter woodland you should keep to the *main* track (50°) at the first Y-junction (both branches here are waymarked). At the next Y-junction after a further 100 yards, you should take the *level, less-used* branch; this is a footpath waymarked with white arrows (the other branch is private). To put all this another way: simply keep right at each of the two Y-junctions.

❹ Stay with the path as it leaves the wood proper and becomes a track running through a narrow band of trees, with fields in view on each side. Immediately after passing under power lines and on re-entering woodland, turn left and leave the wood for a field-corner, taking directions from waymark arrows as before (if you find yourself on a road, you have gone too far!). You should now cross this very large field towards the right-hand side of a distant farm at Rockwell End (360°). Crossing a stile there (well to the left of a pole-mounted transformer) and turning left at a road, soon pass between farm buildings to a road junction.

❺ Keep right at the junction (for Henley)

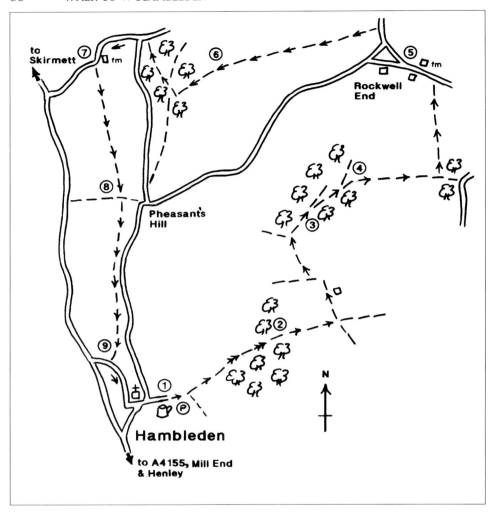

and straight on at the next (for Frieth); then, after 50 yards, leave the road where it curves slightly right. Taking directions from a footpath signpost at this point, cross the left-hand field along an almost level farm track – from which you cannot fail to notice the fine roof-scape of Rockwell End's barns!

❻ After the Hambleden Valley reappears in all its glory, the track leaves this very large field and passes under trees. It eventually drops downhill, turns right and goes over an oblique crossing-path. After turning left onto a road you should ignore Bottom Hill coming in from the left and continue downhill, turning left with the road lower down.

PLACES of INTEREST

Mill End, just a mile's drive away, is an attractive part of the river Thames. Here you can walk a footway across the weir to **Hambleden Lock**. There's a car park on the right prior to the A4155.

❼ When the road soon turns right by Colstrope Farm (not to be confused with Little Colstrope), go through a kissing-gate at the corner and walk a level route through a pasture, passing farm buildings and a pond in the process. Go through another kissing-gate quite soon and follow a right-hand field-edge to a stile in the far corner, ignoring a stile in the hedge en route. Continue forward along the next two fields and meet a drive at the far end, by the houses at Pheasant's Hill. If you divert briefly uphill along the drive, you will discover that here is another attractive Chiltern village!

❽ Back on the path continue in your previous direction, between gardens and into a pasture. From a stile and kissing-gate under a band of tall trees keep forward to another kissing-gate; then ease round to the right when you are halfway along the next pasture, aiming for a kissing-gate at the roadside.

❾ Turning left at the road, and left again into Hambleden's churchyard path, soon emerge at the village square.

Colstrope Farm.

ROTHERFIELD PEPPARD

Length: 4 miles

Getting there: From Nettlebed on the A4130 follow the B481 (Reading direction) for 3 miles to Rotherfield Peppard – which is generally abbreviated to 'Peppard'. This route is through Highmoor Cross and Satwell. You could alternatively approach from Henley, via Greys.

Parking: A good place to park is alongside the common near the Red Lion, where the walk starts. There is also some space 130 yards along the walk, before the road starts to descend.

Maps: OS Explorer 3 Chiltern Hills South or Landranger 175 Reading, Windsor and surrounding area (GR 709819).

Massingham in *Chiltern Country* aptly describes Rotherfield Peppard Common as 'large enough to throw a veil of distance over the kinds of houses that surround it'. The same can be said in terms of the traffic that now crosses it. This 'feld or open land where cattle grazed' is certainly the place to enjoy all-round sky-scapes, as a backcloth to the expanse of grass and the distant houses.

Apart from a ¼ mile moderately steep incline, this walk is to all intents and purposes without hills. So you should not be too exhausted to enjoy two of its best

FOOD and DRINK

You are well supplied with pubs along this walk: the Red Lion and the Dog on Rotherfield Peppard Common and the Lamb at Satwell. The Red Lion offers a wide selection of food, from baguettes and ploughman's at one end of the spectrum to superb Aberdeen Angus steaks at the other. Included on the menu are vegetarian and fish dishes and a mixed grill that would 'defy Desperate Dan'! Telephone: 01491 628329. If you fancy an oriental meal, the Dog has a choice of Thai, Chinese and Indian dishes – in addition to traditional pub meals and snacks. Telephone: 01491 628343. The 1½ mile drive to Rotherfield Greys is well worth making, for that will take you to the Maltsters Arms. Telephone: 01491 628400.

features – Shepherd's Green and Greys Green! Shepherd's Green with its thatched cottages is situated in a peaceful cul-de-sac, while Greys Green, though busy with passing traffic, presents a most pleasing aspect – especially when village cricket is in full swing!

THE WALK

❶ Starting from the Red Lion go along the road (a right turn if leaving the pub) and follow this alongside the common and downhill. When it curves left at the bottom keep forward into a bridleway under trees. In fact you will find two routes running parallel, the right-hand being easier on the feet. The two paths eventually join forces and continue forward as one, while a field comes into view on the right. Leave the wood through a gap and join a path between fields, with a hedge on the immediate right.

❷ After 150 yards the path enters another wood, following its lowest level. Three uphill branching paths (when you are adjacent to the far end of the left-hand field) should be ignored as you continue along the lowest level for another ¼ mile to a major crossing. If there's a field in view half-left from the crossing, you are certainly in the right place!

❸ Turn right at the crossing and go uphill on a track, taking guidance from the white waymark arrows and ignoring a left-hand branch after 20 yards. With fields coming into view again, follow the dip in the wooded hillside and eventually join the B481 at Satwell, by Field House.

❹ Cross the B481 to the lane opposite and go along this to the Lamb, which, if your timing is good, will welcome you inside! Turn left at the road junction by the pub (for Nettlebed) and soon rejoin the B481, leaving this for a signposted path on the right where the roads meet. At least two parallel paths have been worked through the wood here. If however you keep the right-hand field in view and proceed for about 200 yards only, all should be well.

❺ On completing that 200 yard stretch, turn right at a waymarked crossing to a stile and a field. Passing a fenced pit on your right, cross the field to a stile by a wood corner and go forward along a field-edge, with the wood on your immediate right. Continue forward again on reaching the far wood-corner, crossing the 'ankle' of the field to another stile in another field-corner. Then forward yet again to a stile at the far right-hand corner, by a three-way signpost. Keep straight on from the stile – under trees and on a wide path – and soon arrive at Shepherd's Green.

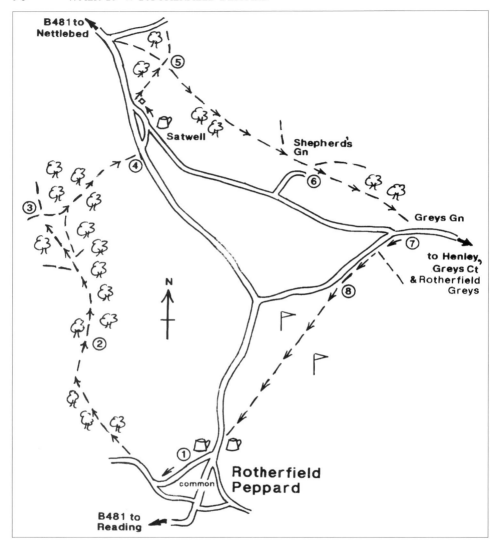

❻ Walk along the left side of the green to where two drives cross obliquely, and join a narrow path running between a field and a garden. You are soon in the field itself, with a hedge on the right, and then on another narrow path, aiming all the while for the right-hand edge of a wood. Go straight on through the wood (parallel to its border) and join a fenced path followed by a rough drive, after which set foot on Greys Green.

❼ Turn right along the road at Greys Green, and, ignoring a branch to Shepherd's Green, walk the grass verge to

PLACES of INTEREST

The National Trust's property **Greys Court**, is 1½ miles from Rotherfield Peppard, near Greys Green. Because of its homely, lived-in atmosphere a visit to the house is a most pleasant experience. It is open to the public from April to September (inclusive) on Monday, Wednesday and Friday afternoons. Teas are also available – which makes a visit even more worth while!

the first bridleway on the left, opposite Pheasant Copse. Go through the gate here and turn right to follow a 'Permissive Bridleway' alongside a hedge and parallel to the road.

❽ On reaching a stile and gate after 220 yards turn half-left into a straight path through young woodland and the golf course greens, passing wooded gardens en route and finally arriving back at Rotherfield Peppard.

Greys Green.

WHITCHURCH

Length: 5½ miles

Getting there:	Pangbourne twice-hourly Monday	pub. There is a telephone box and

Getting there: The nearest main roads are the A329 and A340 at Pangbourne, ½ mile to the south. Join the B471 (Whitchurch Road) from the A329 (Pangbourne High Street) and cross the Thames toll bridge – for a very modest fee! Trains between London (Paddington) and Oxford call at

Pangbourne twice-hourly Monday to Saturday. Alternate trains from London require a change at Reading. The service is hourly on Sunday (change at Reading).

Parking: The best place to park is along Manor Road, which is off the B471, uphill from the Greyhound

pub. There is a telephone box and a signpost to the village hall where Manor Road leaves the B471.

Map: OS Landranger 175 Reading, Windsor and surrounding area (GR 634773).

Where it descends the Chiltern escarpment en route to the river Thames, the long High Street through Whitchurch is graced by a wealth of fine houses and cottages. And where it meets the river the road joins hands with its neighbour Pangbourne, making the link with an attractive toll bridge. Close to the bridge on the Whitchurch side you will find the mill pond, the mill buildings and Church Cottages, which together compose a most delightful scene.

FOOD and DRINK

The Ferryboat Inn at Whitchurch (on the B471 just north of the toll bridge) offers a warm welcome to walkers, children and dogs! It even provides plastic bags for those muddy boots! The menu includes bar snacks (ploughman's, sandwiches and filled jacket potatoes), main meals and puddings. And it's all home-made. Telephone: 01734 842161. The Greyhound (also on the B471) is proud to call itself a traditional English pub, where there are no juke boxes, games machines, background music or 'meals out of a packet'! Telephone: 0118 9842160. In addition to two coffee shop/restaurants and a fish and chip takeaway, nearby Pangbourne has a number of good pubs.

Running parallel to the Thames as far as Gatehampton, the walk offers superb views through gaps in the riverside trees. At Hartslock Nature Reserve a feast of flowers and butterflies (in their season) and a breathtaking view of the Thames and the Thames Valley colour the return journey. From the nature reserve the walk resumes a long, steady climb of the escarpment, before levelling out and descending to Whitchurch.

THE WALK

❶ Assuming you have parked in Manor Road as suggested, leave the road to rejoin Whitchurch High Street (B471). Follow this uphill through the road junction and soon turn left into a gravel drive labelled 'Thames Path', by a speed derestriction sign. Avoiding all branches, follow the drive straight on between fields and trees until it turns left to become a private entrance (Hartslock Farm). Keep forward from this point, down a long flight of steps and into the dip of a magnificent valley.

❷ Pulling out of the dip the path runs between meadows and under trees. It meanders and descends, and becomes a terraced path. It offers 'out of this world' views of the Thames, which flows its parallel course lower down. Basildon Park, a National Trust house open to the public, is also in view – beyond the river's western bank.

❸ On finally leaving the wood, ignore a stile a little uphill on the right – except to note that beyond it lies the Hartslock Nature Reserve. The reserve has 'escaped ploughing and artificial fertilisers' and displays 'an abundance of wildflowers and butterflies'. No need to explore it just yet – there is a better access point later in the walk. Continue forward again, with the river on the left and Gatehampton's houses ahead. Prior to the houses (by about 100 yards) a branching path labelled 'Thames Path' leads to Ferry Cottage and the river – a pleasant diversion and an opportunity to take a break in the walk.

❹ Returning to the previous path and continuing as before, soon arrive at a crossing by Gattendon Lodge. Gatehampton Manor is nearby (to the immediate left), also a particularly fine barn opposite the farmhouse. For a view of the latter keep forward over the crossing for about 100 yards. Back at the crossing and with Gattendon Lodge on your right, go uphill on a shady track and turn right into a lane. Leave the lane when it eventually turns left, and go forward on a track under trees. A stile on the right after 150 yards is the other entrance to Hartslock Nature Reserve. By crossing the stile and climbing the hillside for a short distance you will be

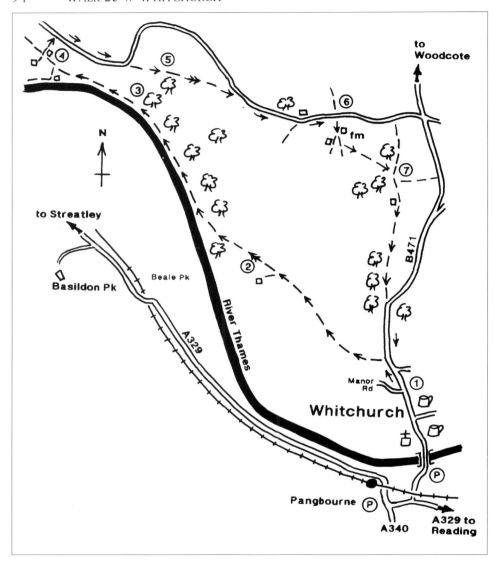

rewarded with a stunning view of the river and the valley. But do please come back!

❺ Back on the track and in the same direction as before, continue along what now becomes a steady uphill path, enjoying a variety of features as you go – meadows, trees, good views and overhead wires! On meeting a lane higher up, go forward along it, eventually passing two cottages on the left, numbered 5 and 6. After a further 200 yards turn right out of the lane (by a pole-

Whitchurch Mill.

PLACES of INTEREST

There is good **riverside walking** (and good places to sit!) on the Pangbourne side of the Thames. Access to the river bank is via a small car park near the southern end of the toll bridge. The National Trust's **Basildon Park** (the house) is well worth a visit and can be approached from the A329 midway between Pangbourne and Streatley. It is open to the public on Wednesday to Sunday afternoons from April to October inclusive. **Beale Park** (the Child Beale Wildlife Trust) is near Basildon Park, on the Thames side of the A329. This is a good place for all the family, but perhaps not after a 5½ mile walk!

mounted transformer) into a rough drive.

❻ The drive is signposted as a footpath to Whitchurch (1 mile). Passing a farmhouse quite soon, take a left-hand branch in the drive and continue for a further 80 yards to a stile and field on the left, opposite the barns of Coombe End Farm. With further buildings over to your right, cross the field-corner half-right to another stile; then continue in the same direction (120°) across two more fields, eventually entering a wood.

❼ Ignore paths coming in from the left as you proceed through the wood; and on entering a pasture keep straight on towards the left side of Beech Farm, now residential. Cross a drive by the 'farm' entrance and go along a swathe of grass (to the left of a hedge) to a kissing-gate. Continue forward across more grass and soon join a path, and after that the right-hand edge of a very large field, with a wood on the immediate right. From a kissing-gate in the far corner of the field (where the electricity wires are heading) go down a short path to the Whitchurch road. On reaching the war memorial cross the road to a raised path opposite and follow this into Whitchurch.

ARGUING DEVELOPMENT POLICY:
Frames and Discourses